Primary School

The ability to use research to inform and improve practice is now a requirement of all teachers. *Primary School Physical Education* presents research evidence about a range of important topics for the primary school teacher of physical education, bringing together a collection of current research data with practical implications. The relevance of research to the teacher is also discussed, including the implications for practice and the ways in which teachers can benefit from access to research evidence.

The topics discussed include:

- policy, practice and prospects for National Curriculum physical education
- physical education and health-promoting primary schools
- using research to inform curriculum planning
- safe practice in primary school physical education
- girls' experience of physical education
- issues related to making physical education genuinely inclusive through considering the needs of Muslim women

Primary School Physical Education illustrates how a wide range of different research approaches can help teachers make sense of their practice or take it forward. It will prove invaluable to practising teachers and students.

Anne Williams is Head of the School of Education at King Alfred's College of Higher Education. She has published extensively on physical education and teacher education and is currently researching girls' experience of National Curriculum physical education.

Primary School Physical Education

Research into Practice

Edited by Anne Williams

London and New York

First published in 2000
by RoutledgeFalmer Press
11 New Fetter Lane, London EC4P 4EE

Simultaneously published in the USA and Canada
by RoutledgeFalmer Press
29 west 35th Street, New York, NY 10001

RoutledgeFalmer Press is an imprint of the Taylor & Francis Group

Typeset in Goudy by Taylor & Francis Books Ltd
Printed and bound in Great Britain by MPG Books Ltd, Bodmin

British Library Cataloguing in Publication Data
A catalogue record for this book is available from the British Library

Library of Congress Cataloging in Publication Data
Williams, Anne (Anne Elizabeth), 1947–
Primary School physical education/Anne Williams.
p. cm.
Includes bibliographical references and index.
1. Physical education and training–Study and teaching (Elementary)
2. Physical education for children. I. Title.

GV443 . W535 2000
372.86–dc21   99–053844

ISBN 0-750-70971-5 (hbk)
ISBN 0-750-70970-7 (pbk)

Contents

Contents

Illustrations

Preface

This book brings together a collection of papers written by teachers and teacher educators with a deep commitment to high-quality and equitable experiences in physical education for primary school children. It has been put together ten years after the publication of *Issues in Physical Education for the Primary Years* (Williams 1989), which, for almost the first time, brought together writings from a range of disciplines and interests, specifically focused upon the primary age range. Given the pace and extent of educational change in the intervening period, it is perhaps surprising that other texts have not appeared to provide primary school teachers with ready access to the relevant research and knowledge which must underpin good practice. The current emphasis on teaching as a research-based profession and the many requests to provide a follow-up to *Issues in Physical Education* have combined to provide the impetus to produce this book.

The primary school years are the key period for physical education, and the relative lack of research interest in this age group in no way reflects the significance of the physical education experiences which children have at primary school. Increasingly, for the talented performer, the foundations for future excellence will have been laid and development will be well under way, particularly in some sports such as gymnastics and swimming. More important for the teacher, the quality of experience provided for all children is key to their subsequent attitude to and learning in and through physical education. Increased emphasis on the need for healthy and active lifestyles underlines further the importance of relevant, positive and inclusive physical education programmes for all children.

The contributors to this book draw on a range of disciplines and personal experience to provide chapters that support healthy, safe and inclusive practice, based upon relevant research evidence. Issues related to healthy active lifestyles are addressed in the context of the individual child by Mike Sleap and his co-authors in Chapter 3, and at the school level by Sue Piotrowski in Chapter 4. Inclusivity is addressed as a National Curriculum issue by Dawn Penney and John Evans in Chapter 2, in the context of gender by Julie Bedward and Anne Williams in Chapter 7, and in relation to ethnicity by Tansin Benn in Chapter

8. Safe practice is considered by Carole Raymond in Chapter 6. The book begins with some discussion of the importance of research to the primary school teacher, and the theme of teacher as researcher is revisited by Gill Bailey and Jes Woodhouse in Chapter 5.

The many pressures on the primary curriculum, and the growing evidence that many subjects are being squeezed for time to create space for the increased emphasis on literacy and numeracy, make it all the more important that all teachers understand the importance of physical education. It is also imperative that there is a good understanding of the sorts of practice that will create learning opportunities for all children irrespective of physical attributes and abilities. This book is a contribution to the creation of that understanding.

Anne Williams
Winchester
July 1999

Reference

Williams, A. (1989) *Issues in Physical Education for the Primary Years*. Brighton: Falmer Press.

1 Research and the Primary School Teacher

Anne Williams

Introduction

The relationship between research, teachers and teaching is, periodically, the subject of lively debate. Within physical education, concerns about research have centred upon its relevance to teachers' day-to-day work, laying a significant part of the blame for its apparent inability to change practice at the door of an over-reliance upon pseudo-scientific approaches to the analysis of teaching and learning (Kirk and Tinning 1990; Schempp 1987). Current issues about educational research in general echo this concern about the relevance of research to teachers' daily practice and the extent to which research informs it (Hargreaves 1996), and also questions the quality of much of the educational research carried out in higher education (Pring 1995; Tooley and Darby 1998), the capacity of educational research to influence policy (Hillage et al. 1998) and the nature and purpose of such research (Ranson 1996).

This chapter will explore the nature of research in so far as it is relevant to the primary school teacher of physical education and will then discuss ways in which teachers might relate to research both as research consumers and as research creators. Some examples, including a number from elsewhere in this book, will be given of specific projects or approaches to research which have the potential to inform the primary school teacher's work in physical education. Finally I will consider the potential of action research to offer an approach which is manageable and relevant to the primary school teacher who wishes to engage in investigative work of his or her own.

What Is Educational Research For?

Much has been made, recently, of the perceived irrelevance of research to classroom practice. Hargreaves (1996), Tooley and Darby (1998) and Hillage et al (1998) have all commented critically about the impact of educational research on the day-to-day practice of teachers. They imply that research that does little to change practice is of no value. One solution proposed, and championed by the Teacher Training Agency,[1] has been to involve teachers more in the research process, as people who do research, rather than as people who have

1

research done 'to them', 'for them', or 'on them'. This suggestion assumes that the critics are correct in their conclusion that current research lacks practical application. As we will see later, many examples may be found of research that does inform practice, although it is often made accessible to teachers via an intermediary – higher education tutor, local education authority adviser or other agent involved in teacher education. It also implies that teachers are not currently involved in research.

The reality, of course, is that many teachers are already engaged in research, albeit on a small scale. Much of this research is undertaken as part of professional development courses, as projects, assignments or dissertations. It tends to be small-scale, local and focused upon an aspect of the teacher's current practice. For many teachers, particularly those following undergraduate training programmes, this process starts during their initial training, part of which involves investigating some aspect of professional practice, often as a final-year project or dissertation. Moreover, much small-scale research undertaken by higher education staff, while not necessarily disseminated nationally, is nevertheless used to inform the day-to-day practice of teaching student teachers or teachers on professional development programmes.

Researchers involved in larger-scale national projects have argued that their role is to provide evidence for use by policy makers, not to act as a pressure group on behalf of their own findings. They absolve themselves, with some justification, for the failure of others to take serious note of the evidence they present. For example, there is a considerable body of evidence to suggest that team games are the preferred activity choice of only a small minority of pupils and are actively disliked by significant numbers of girls, yet it is questionable whether the failure of physical education policy to take this evidence on board can be blamed on those who produced the evidence and passed it on to those responsible for policy development. Team games have been emphasized within the national curriculum for physical education in spite of the availability of evidence suggesting that they have limited appeal to many pupils, particularly adolescent girls, not because there was no evidence available. The proposed removal of the requirement to continue to include games as a curriculum activity at Key Stage 4 (QCA 1999), while welcome, does not actually address the issue of relevance of games at Key Stage 3 for many adolescent girls.

Current criticism thus seems to focus on quality, scale and relevance. What is the primary school teacher to make of this? Does research have to be large-scale in order to be high quality or in order to be relevant? On the face of it, it seems unlikely that many teachers will be in a position to acquire easily the knowledge and skills to address all the quality issues or that many would be able to undertake work on a large scale. It can, however, be argued that research which informs teaching is often most effective and certainly most likely to be perceived as relevant if it is local and relatively small-scale. To give a personal example: I was able to use data gathered for my own higher degree with my initial teacher training students for several years. The fact that the data came from the schools in which the students were undertaking their placements gave it a relevance and an immediacy which a national project simply did not have.

One reason for some of the confusion which exists currently is, arguably, a failure to clarify the nature and purpose of educational research. This inevitably leads to judgements being made about research using criteria related to research with quite different aims. Ranson (1996) quotes Rosemary Deem's succinct analysis of this division, characterized as a 'split between those wanting research to be relevant directly to practice and those wanting to make a theoretical and empirical contribution to knowledge'. Bassey defines research as simply the search for knowledge.

> In carrying out research the purpose is to try to make some claim to knowledge; to try to show something that was not known before. However small, however modest the hoped for claim to knowledge is, provided it is carried out systematically, critically and self-critically, the search for knowledge is research.
>
> (Bassey 1990)

If this definition is accepted then many examples may be found of individual efforts that may quite legitimately be described as research, albeit small-scale and limited in scope. Such a definition validates claims that all teachers can or should be researchers. It also has the potential to encompass a diverse range of research methodologies arising from a range of paradigms within which individuals or research groups locate themselves. Sparkes (1992) notes the advocacy of alternative approaches to research in physical education that bring with them a challenge to the historical dominance of the empirical paradigm. Some (Kirk and Tinning 1990) would probably argue that the challenge has had only limited success although Dodds (1999) claims that at least three paradigms – positivist, interpretive and critical pedagogy – are thriving. Sparkes defines a paradigm as a belief system, involving sets of values and assumptions which individuals adopt with respect to the research enterprise, and which are products of their personal life histories. Different paradigms lead to different approaches, methods and outcomes and thus to the possibility of qualitatively different impact upon practice. The next section will look at how these variations manifest themselves in the context of primary school physical education.

What Sort of Research?

Changes in approaches to the study of physical education and allied subjects – sports studies, sports science, human movement studies and so on – over the past twenty years have seen a steady movement towards aspects of the subject related to physical science and away from those elements which have their base in social science. Kirk and Tinning have been highly critical of the trend towards the privileging of knowledge that derives from 'hard' science, and of the

3

dominance of scientism or scientific functionalism both in physical education and, more generally, in Western society (Kirk and Tinning 1990). Schempp (1989) questions the reliance on the natural science paradigm, which he claims has become the dominant approach to research on physical education teaching. Kirk (1989) suggests that it is these very approaches which lead to criticism from teachers that research and theory are remote from their day-to-day practice, and largely irrelevant to them. All argue for more emphasis upon approaches to research that are more socially critical, qualitative and eclectic, while Dodds (1999) suggests that recent progress towards more varied approaches is encouraging.

Undoubtedly, different research traditions can offer qualitatively different information to the teacher, as the examples later in this chapter show. Physical education has historically had close links with life sciences, through the study of, for example, exercise physiology, motor development and sport psychology. Empirical evidence, located within a positivist paradigm in these areas, offers the teacher important information, highly relevant to day-to-day practice. For example, empirical research has shown that the child's response to exercise is qualitatively different from that of the adult, and, thus their exercise needs are different. It has provided important information about the developmental process that the young child goes through in learning motor skills. Perhaps not surprisingly, physical education researchers initially adopted a positivist paradigm and empirical methodology for curriculum-focused work. This approach provided a range of information: some has impacted upon practice, but, arguably, was too narrow in focus to fulfil the potential of curriculum-focused work to change practice. Sparkes' advocacy of alternative approaches recognizes that a more varied approach may lead to increased research impact.

Choice of research approach depends partly on the aspect of physical education to be investigated and partly upon individual views of the nature of the work being studied. These choices are often polarized as positivist–interpretative, quantitative–qualitative or objective–subjective. The positivist sees the world as paralleling the world of natural phenomena. That is, it has an objective reality, measurable and capable of analysis through surveys or experimental work. Examples from physical education would include the use of attitude scales to measure children's perceptions of physical education or the use of surveys to ascertain teacher's views about the importance of physical education within the primary school curriculum. Such work tends to be quantitative and concerned with measurement of the incidence of particular features or analysis of relationships between variables. Conclusions might be that teachers with specialist training see physical education as more important than those with only a basic preparation or that boys view physical education more positively than girls.

The alternative view emphasizes the importance of the subjective experience of individuals and the creation of the social world. A key concern is how the individual creates, modifies and interprets the world in which she or he finds him or herself.

A key issue for all educational research, including that related to physical education, is that of its relevance to, and use by teachers. A number of writers (Bassey 1994; Elliott 1991; McNiff 1988; Kirk 1989) see action research as an important means of involving teachers in research as active participants rather than as subjects who have research 'done to them'. We will return to the issue of action research after consideration of some research which has the potential to inform the primary school teacher's practice.

The Teacher as Research Consumer

There are various ways in which different kinds of research can help the primary school teacher to reflect on and develop provision in physical education. We will look here at a selection that varies in scale, purpose and approach. They range in scale from national projects, undertaken over a long period producing data and interpretations which have been validated and tested for reliability, to small-scale local projects, involving a single teacher's analysis of an aspect of her work with one class of children.

If research is a search for knowledge then its outcomes can serve the teacher in a number of ways. Knowledge can lead to informed action, to an increased ability to inform and advise others, or to better informed choice. The knowledge generated by the research may relate to the children and their needs, whether within the physical education curriculum or in relation to other physical activity in which they may be involved. It may relate to the context in which they live, or in which their learning takes place, and, as such, help the teacher to plan more effectively in relation to their needs. It may relate to the school and the curriculum and may enable the teacher to plan physical education provision to maximize its contribution, not only to the physical growth, development and learning of the children, but also to other aspects of the primary school educational process.

There is now a considerable body of research that can inform us about how children grow and develop and about how they learn physical skills. Research tells us about children's physical response to exercise and how this differs from the response of adults. It tells us about the processes of skill learning and about factors that can enhance or inhibit the learning of physical skills. There is a growing body of evidence about children's activity lifestyles (Armstrong et al. 1998; Cale 1996; Warburton and Woods 1996) both in and out of school. All the evidence suggests that children are less active than they should be in terms of general lifestyle (Armstrong et al. 1998) and that physical education lessons are insufficiently active to contribute to long-term health (Warburton and Woods 1996). This is valuable information for teachers, but raises many questions about how they should respond. Chapter 3 of this book provides further insights into this issue. It suggests that while some of the concern expressed about children's sedentary lifestyles may be misconceived, encouraging physically active lifestyles remains important.

Other research on children and physical activity is related to growth and development. For example Aldridge (1993) describes research undertaken in the 1960s that revealed different patterns of the development of skeletal maturity among children involved in different sports, with gymnasts showing a tendency towards an immature physique, in contrast to swimmers who tend to be skeletally advanced. The researchers conclude that the sports-specific relationship between skeletal development and success is unlikely to be due to the training required for different sports, but is more likely to be an inherited characteristic in the individual. This kind of knowledge can help the teacher to understand the performance levels achieved by gifted pupils in their classes as well as to appreciate possible reasons for children giving up a sport at which they appear to excel.

Such knowledge is also important if the teacher is to appreciate the potential risks to the primary school child of too much pressure to participate and compete. While good advice should be available to parents and children through well trained coaches, the pressures on talented youngsters to train and play to excess remain. Over-use injuries among able young footballers, for example, continue to appear. The teacher may be well placed to advise parents and children if he or she is aware that playing matches at weekends as well as for the school may not be in the long-term physical interests of the individual and is able to explain to parents some of the physiological consequences of placing excessive demands on an immature physique.

Research into the ways in which children learn physical skills is also valuable for the teacher. Connell (1993) emphasizes the need for the coach to adopt a style that takes into account children's thinking and learning abilities and the same is just as true for the teacher in the school context. Mosston's work on teaching styles offers some insights into how the teaching style adopted can impact upon the learning outcomes (Mosston and Ashworth 1986).

Research into pupils' attitudes towards physical education can provide the teacher with important information about factors which affect attitudes. This research has tended to be focused upon the secondary rather than the primary age range, but even here, there are lessons for the primary school teacher. Figley (1985) uses critical incident technique to collect data about persons, places, conditions or activities that have turned pupils off physical education. She classifies the responses into teacher, curriculum, atmosphere, self-perception, peer behaviour and other, as attitude determinants. Luke and Sinclair (1991) produce a similar classification – teacher, curriculum, atmosphere, self-perception and other, but add facilities as a further factor. Williams and Bedward (1999) confirm these classifications in general terms, categorizing pupils' feelings as influenced by the activity offered, the learning context (mixed/single sex, weather conditions, uniform rules, showering procedures), student's ability/self-concept, peer attitude and teacher style/teacher attitude. Chapter 7 explores some of the implications of Williams and Bedward's work for the primary school teacher.

Equally relevant is research that illustrates the different ways in which children may be motivated to achieve in physical education and suggests that the teacher needs to ensure that his or her practice will motivate children with different perspectives on performance. Two distinctive approaches can be identified in relation to ways in which children measure their achievement. Children with a mastery goal perspective are concerned with demonstrating mastery of a task, while children with a competitive goal perspective are concerned with demonstrating ability compared to others (Dweck 1986, Ames 1984). Ewing (1981) and, more recently, Buchan and Roberts (1991) related these orientations to the age of children, demonstrating that younger children tend not to have a fully developed competitive goal perspective, and Roberts (1992) notes that the motivational climate created by adults, including teachers, can influence the development of one goal perspective rather than another. Clearly a group of children whose focus is on mastery of a task will be better placed to maintain high levels of motivation and therefore high achievement and improvement levels than those whose focus is on their performance in relation to that of others, and who will, in consequence become discouraged easily if they appear to be failing. Given that there is considerable evidence to suggest that children do not differentiate between skill, effort and ability until around the age of 12, the primary school teacher is well placed to maintain high levels of motivation through the judicious use of feedback which encourages a continued focus on mastery rather than on competition.

Research can also provide the teacher with evidence to substantiate what may be apparent at a common-sense or personal observation level. Reference to relevant research evidence may be useful in persuading others of the need to change practice or to adopt or avoid particular procedures. For example Evans (1985) demonstrates that, among 8–12-year-olds, selection of teams tends to follow a strict hierarchy based upon ability, ensuring that the least able are picked last or excluded altogether. Children with poor physical skills are frequently denied access to games in progress (Evans and Roberts 1987), are less likely to have good relations with their peers and are disadvantaged when trying to establish friendships. This evidence underlines the need for the teacher to be sensitive to ways in which physical education experiences can affect self-esteem and, as a consequence, some social relationships. In particular there is the need to eliminate some quite common practices such as allowing children to pick teams, or to provide clear ground rules and guidance to ensure that low-ability children are not excluded.

Children grow up as members of particular communities and cultures. In Chapter 9 we can see how research into the experiences of members of a particular Asian community can help teachers in schools and colleges to offer a relevant and accessible curriculum. This is another example where the use teachers might make of the research evidence would depend upon the context in which they were working. There is much of direct practical use for the teacher who is working in a school where some or many of the pupils are

Muslim. Equally, the teacher working in an all-white school, or one where the cultural and ethnic mix is different, could learn much about the needs of groups which tend to be under-represented in physical education and sport.

Hopkins and Putnam (1993) provide a case study of adventure education provision in a middle school. In describing the purpose, the programme and the outcomes, they offer the teacher some insight into why a particular school has been successful in promoting this particular activity area. Given that primary schools are likely to be able to choose, in the future, whether to offer this activity or not, at Key Stage 2 (Casbon 1999), such information can help in the process of deciding whether an individual school is in a position to provide the kind of context and expertise in which adventurous activities could flourish.

Chapter 4 looks at evidence about the individual school's contribution to the promotion of health and, specifically, at the extent to which physical education was able to play a part. This is another example of the case study approach, which can be the basis of changed practice within the schools involved, but which may also be useful to other schools who are reviewing their own practice.

One of the most comprehensive sources of evidence about teaching and learning in schools is the Ofsted database. Whether the Ofsted process meets the standards expected of national-level research in terms of conventional expectations of objectivity, reliability or validity is open to question, not least because of the large number of people involved in making judgements about teaching and learning in schools. Nevertheless it is a substantial body of data, including information about the teaching and learning of physical education in every primary school in the country, and additional evidence has been collected to produce a summary of what characterizes good practice in physical education (Ofsted 1995). While this survey contains more about secondary than about primary school physical education, it does contain a number of statements about specific factors which characterize good practice in the primary school. For example, 'Effective co-ordination of the subject was best achieved when the headteacher was enthusiastic about physical education and provided support for the subject co-ordinator' (Ofsted 1985: 3).

This underlines the importance of good communication between head-teacher and subject co-ordinator and suggests that a newly appointed co-ordinator needs to spend time ensuring the headteacher understands and supports his or her plans and priorities. The publication also provides some useful benchmarks against which co-ordinators or class teachers could judge their own work.

With respect to time allocation,

> Most pupils had between 8% and 10% of the week for physical education lessons. The primary schools had well-balanced programmes with weekly lessons providing a strong focus on games, gymnastics and dance.... All the schools gave generous attention to swimming.
>
> (Ofsted 1995: 13)

The survey also provides some examples of good practice which other schools might wish to emulate:

> Both the headteacher and the co-ordinator taught demonstration lessons, assisted with planning or taught alongside teachers who were less confident. The headteacher bought in supply cover to release the co-ordinator from classteacher duties in order to allow this development to be extended. The headteacher who is himself an outstandingly good practitioner in the teaching of physical education gives initial support – by teaching for and with the teacher – to every new appointee, in order to ensure that the well-established and shared practices of all staff are fully understood and that the standard of work is consistently high throughout the school.
>
> (Ofsted 1995: 16)

Individual reports obviously provide a certain amount of evidence about practice in a specific school. The easy availability of schools reports via the internet (www.ofsted.gov.uk) means that the teacher has ready access to evidence about physical education in other schools in the immediate locality or within a cluster of similar schools.

In summary then, research can:

- provide information about children's growth and development that can enable the teacher to understand better why some activities and some levels of activity could be prejudicial to the individual child;
- provide information about the exercise and activity needs and levels of particular populations;
- provide information about children's attitudes to activity in general and towards specific activities, together with reasons for particular activities and preferences;
- provide information about children's motivation which can help the teacher to plan their teaching for the inclusion of the maximum number of children;
- provide information about factors which contribute to good practice in physical education provision;
- provide information about ways in which the backgrounds of individual pupils or groups can impact upon their participation and learning in physical education;
- provide information about ways in which teachers can work in order to bring about more effective learning;
- provide information about practice in other schools.

The Primary School Teacher as Researcher

All the examples so far are of research done on children, schools or teachers, with, for the most part, minimal involvement of the teacher. The teacher has little or no control over the research process. As Walker (1985) notes, such research is more correctly described as 'research on education' rather than being integral to the pursuit of schools' or teachers' concerns. A variety of initiatives has attempted to involve teachers much more centrally as researchers in their own schools. Much of this work comes under the heading of 'action research', which involves a commitment by teachers to investigate and reflect upon their own practice and has its roots in the curriculum development and research movement of the early 1970s (Stenhouse 1975). Action research is generally based upon cycles that include key elements: planning; action; review; revision; further action. This kind of cycle can be repeated once or many times. Many action research models build in the possibility of reviewing and changing the initial idea in the light of experience (Bassey 1994). However, for many teachers, with limited time and concerned about a highly specific issue in a particular time and context, this may not be appropriate. It is partly for this reason that the term 'practitioner research' is used to describe the kind of research that teachers reading this book might embark on. The Open University (1991) uses the term 'practitioner research' to describe research conducted by teachers in their own classrooms, but implying a rather more inclusive and eclectic approach than that of action research. As the Open University writers note, action research has a range of advocates who all define its nature and processes slightly differently; most of them describe a process which has a fairly long time scale and which requires the completion of certain key components generally represented by either a flow chart or spiral diagram.

Elliott (1991) describes the purpose of action research as the improvement of practice rather than the production of knowledge. That is, rather than seeking knowledge which may or may not be used subsequently to influence practice, the primary aim of action or practitioner research is change in order to improve some element of practice. Cohen and Manion (1989) describe it as 'essentially an on the spot procedure designed to deal with a concrete problem located in an immediate situation'. Practitioner research thus avoids the criticism of other educational research, namely its failure to influence policy or practice, by placing change in classroom practice at the heart of the research process. A number of questions should be asked of such research: some would apply to any work undertaken; the relevance of others would be dependent upon the purpose of the research. What is important is that the work the teacher does is fit for the purpose: that is, it serves the need it has been planned to meet. Many teachers would say that they do not have the skills to be researchers and would see research as the province of academics employed in higher education or of research professionals. Most would, however, probably be quite prepared to admit that they are involved in study, investigation or enquiry from time to time. Some would argue that this is not the same as engagement with research, but I would agree with Bell (1993) that using these terms interchangeably is quite legitimate and with Howard and Sharp (1983), who state:

> Many people associate the word 'research' with activities which are substantially removed from day to day life and which are pursued by outstandingly gifted persons with an unusual level of commitment. There is of course, a good deal of truth in this viewpoint, but we would argue that the pursuit is not restricted to this type of person and indeed can prove to be a stimulating and satisfying experience for many people with a trained and enquiring mind.
>
> (Howard and Sharp, 1983: 6)

As Tinning (1992) notes, action research did not feature highly in physical education research before the 1990s. In one of few published pieces to focus upon action research in the physical education context, Kirk (1995) identifies six key features that he claims are characteristic of action research which can contribute to the improvement of practice:

- action research is collaborative, in that, while it is possible for individuals to investigate their practice on their own it is likely that there will be greater benefits in terms of effectiveness, understanding and change when people who share a common interest or who are each affected by a physical education or sport programme participate together in action research;
- action research is participatory and self-managed, that is, the research agenda is controlled by the people whose practices are the topic of enquiry so that it provides outcomes which are meaningful and beneficial to all participants;
- action research is data based, that is, it is not simply what teachers normally do when they teach in that it involves the systematic collection of information on which to base reflection and action;
- action research involves reflection, that is an active process of engaging intellectually with information about the topic under investigation;
- action research is situated, that is it involves looking in on practice and, at the same time, looking out to see where those practices are located along-side or within other, broader social and educational practices;
- action research is reform-oriented, that is it is justified on the basis of its practical consequences, rather than being research for the sake of doing research.

Most of these would be accepted by other advocates of action research. For example, Denscombe (1998) characterizes action research as practical, including change as an integral part, involving a cyclical process and seeing practitioners as crucial active participants. Zuber-Skerritt's definition involves a cyclical process of strategic planning, action, observation and critical and self-critical reflection on the results of the preceding strategies (Zuber-Skerritt 1996). McNiff (1988), while not disputing either of these, is less prescriptive, seeing action research as a way of characterizing a loose set of activities that are designed to improve the quality of education.

Chapter 5 is an example of practitioner research, on a small scale, prompted by one teacher's need to make informed decisions in relation to her curriculum planning. In addition to describing the process and the benefits which accrued, this chapter highlights the need for appropriate support if individual teacher effort is to be successful and supports Kirk's claims that action research should be collaborative. In this case the support came from outside the school. Other teachers might find the necessary support by working as a group within their schools, by collaborating with other schools in their cluster or pyramid or through linking such work to a professional development course which can also offer support and guidance.

For example, a group of teachers might work together in a primary school cluster in order to develop strategies for overcoming the negative attitudes of some boys towards dance in the physical education curriculum. Evidence might involve talking to groups of boys about their perceptions of dance as a subject area, particular likes and dislikes, involvement in dance or related activities outside school. Action might involve changing the content of lessons or the way in which teaching is organized. For example, two classes might be time-tabled simultaneously so that single-sex teaching groups become a possibility. The effect of these changes would be monitored, discussed and further action planned – either to adopt a particular strategy across the whole cluster if it had been seen to be effective, or to try different strategies if there was evidence that the first interventions had not been successful.

Summary

The teacher should therefore be a user of research, and may well wish to be a creator, albeit in a small way. The boundary between reflective practice and research is not clear and there are various contradictory views about where it should be drawn. If teaching is to be seen as a research-based profession, there are strong arguments for definitions of research that are inclusive as possible, with differences defined in terms of scale and purpose, rather than in ways which exclude most teachers from what is seen as an exclusive community. By making effective use of research evidence already in the public domain, the teacher can be confident that practice is based upon current knowledge of the various issues which impact upon the child's learning. Personal engagement in research such as action research on a modest scale offers further opportunities for individual teachers to continue to develop practice based upon critical and informed analysis of their working context.

Note

1   The Teacher Training Agency was set up as a government quango in 1993, initially with responsibility for funding and allocation of numbers to initial teacher training, but subsequently with a much expanded brief which included recruitment, professional standards, continuing professional development and a limited involvement with research. Its remit was narrowed once more following a government review in 1999.

References

Aldridge, J. (1993) 'Skeletal growth and development', in M. Lee (ed.) *Coaching Children in Sport*. London: E & F Spon.

Ames, C. (1984) 'Competitive, co-operative and individualistic goal structures: a cognitive-motivational analysis', in R. Ames and C. Ames (eds) *Research on Motivation in Education, Vol. 1: Student motivation*. New York: Academic Press.

Armstrong, N., Welsman, J., and Kirby, B. (1998) 'Aerobic exercise and physical activity patterns of young people', in K. Green and K. Hardman (eds) *Physical Education: A reader*. Oxford: Meyer and Meyer.

Bassey, M. (1990) 'On the nature of research in education (part 1), *Research Intelligence*. BERA Newsletter No. 36, Summer, 35–8.

——(1994) *Action Research for Primary School Teachers*. Newark: Michael Bassey.

Bell, J. (1993) *Doing Your Research Project*. Buckingham: Open University Press.

Buchan, F. and Roberts, G.C. (1991) 'Perceptions of success of children in sport'. Unpublished manuscript, University of Illinois. Cited in M. Lee (ed.) *Coaching Children in Sport*. London: E & F Spon.

Cale, L. (1996) 'An assessment of the physical activity levels of adolescent girls – implications for physical education, *European Journal of Physical Education* 1, 1, 46–55.

Casbon, C. (1999) 'National Curriculum Review Update – Key Points in the Review of the Order, *British Journal of Physical Education* 29, 1, 6–7.

Cohen, L. and Manion, L. (1994) *Research Methods in Education*, 4th edn. London: Routledge.

Connell, R. (1993) 'Understanding the learner: guidelines for the coach'. In M. Lee (ed.) *Coaching Children in Sport*. London: E & F Spon.

Denscombe, M. (1998) *The Good Research Guide*. Buckingham: Open University Press.

Dodds, P. (1999) 'Silver bullets, golden visions and possible dreams: a wish list for the future of research in physical education', in C.A. Hardy and M. Mawer (eds) *Learning and Teaching in Physical Education*. London: Falmer Press.

Dweck, C.S. (1986) 'Motivational processes affecting learning', *American Psychologist* 41, 1040–8.

Elliott, J. (1991) *Action Research for Educational Change*. Milton Keynes: Open University Press.

Evans, J. (1985) 'The process of team selection in children's self-directed and adult-directed games', PhD Dissertation, University of Illinois.

Evans, J. and Roberts, G.C. (1987) 'Physical competence and the development of children's peer relations', *Quest* 39, 23–35.

Ewing, M.E. (1981) 'Achievement orientations and sports behavior in males and females', PhD Dissertation, University of Illinois. Cited in M. Lee (ed.) *Coaching Children in Sport*. London: E & F Spon.

13

Figley, G. (1985) 'Determinants of attitudes towards physical education', *Journal of Teaching in Physical Education* 4, 229–40.

Hargreaves, D. (1996) 'Teaching as a research-based profession: possibilities and prospects', TTA Annual Lecture, 1996.

Hillage, J., Pearson, R., Anderson, A. and Tamkin, P. (1998) *Excellence in Research on Schools*, Research Report No 74. London: DfEE.

Hopkins, D. and Putnam, R. (1993) *Personal Growth Through Adventure*. London: David Fulton.

Howard, K. and Sharp, J.A. (1983) *The Management of a Student Research Project*. Aldershot: Gower.

Kirk, D. (1989) 'The orthodoxy in RT-PE and the research/practice gap: a critique and an alternative view', *Journal of Teaching in Physical Education* 8, 123–30.

—— (1995) 'Action research and educational reform in physical education', *Pedagogy in Practice* 1, 1, 4–21.

Kirk, D. and Tinning, R. (1990) *Physical Education, Curriculum and Culture*. Basingstoke: Falmer Press.

Kremer, J., Trew, K. and Ogle, S. (1997) *Young People's Involvement in Sport*. London: Routledge.

Lee, M. (ed.) *Coaching Children in Sport*. London: E & F Spon.

Luke, M.D. and Sinclair, G.D. (1991) 'Gender differences in adolescents' attitudes towards school physical education', *Journal of Teaching in Physical Education* 11, 31–46.

McNiff, J. (1988) *Action Research: Principles and practice*. London: Routledge.

Mosston, M. and Ashworth, S. (1986) *Teaching Physical Education*, 3rd edn. Columbus: Merrill Publishing.

Ofsted (1995) *Physical Education and Sport in Schools: A survey of good practice*. London: HMSO.

Open University (1991) *Professional Development in Action: Methodology handbook*. Milton Keynes: Open University Press.

Pring, R. (1995) Editorial, *British Journal of Educational Studies* 42, 2, 121–4.

QCA (1999) *The Review of the National Curriculum in England; The consultation materials*. London: QCA.

Ranson, S. (1996) 'The future of education research: learning at the centre', *British Educational Research Journal* 22, 5, 523–35.

Roberts, G.C. (ed.) (1992) *Motivation in Sport and Exercise*. Champaign, IL: Human Kinetics.

Schempp, P. (1987) 'Research on teaching in physical education: beyond the limits of natural science', *Journal of Teaching in Physical Education* 6, 111–21.

Sparkes, A. (1992) (ed.) *Research in Physical Education and Sport: Exploring alternative visions*. Brighton: Falmer Press.

Stenhouse, L. (1975) *An Introduction to Curriculum Research and Development*. London: Heinemann Education.

Tinning, R. (1992) 'Action research as epistemology and practice: towards transformative educational practice in physical education', in A. Sparkes (ed.) *Research in Physical Education and Sport: Exploring alternative visions*. Brighton: Falmer Press.

Tooley, J. and Darby, D. (1998) *Educational Research: A critique*. London: Ofsted.

Walker, R. (1985) *Doing Research: A handbook for teachers*. London: Routledge.

Warburton, P. and Woods, J. (1996) 'Observation of children's physical activity levels during primary school physical education lessons', *European Journal of Physical Education* 1, 1, 56–65.

Williams, E.A. and Bedward, J. (1999) *Games for the Girls: The impact of recent policy on the provision of physical education and sporting opportunities for female adolescents*. Report to the Nuffield Foundtion. Winchester: King Alfred's College.

Zuber-Skerritt, O. (1996) (ed.) *New Directions in Action Research*, London: Falmer.

www.ofsted.gov.uk.

2 The National Curriculum for Physical Education

Policy, Practice and Prospects

Dawn Penney and John Evans

Introduction: Researching Policy, Developing Practice

In this chapter we draw on research that since 1990 has sought to monitor and critique the ongoing development and implementation of the National Curriculum for Physical Education (NCPE) in England and Wales. During this time, as teachers in schools, we have faced the far from easy task of attempting to keep pace with developments, and also a need to be somewhat selective in our focus. As a result, our research has engaged more with the secondary than the primary sector. Nevertheless, we have endeavoured (albeit with reference to a necessarily limited number of schools; see Evans et al. 1996), to identify and address a number of key issues arising for primary schools and teachers within them as they have sought to respond to the introduction of an NCPE. In all of our research we have been particularly concerned to pursue the complexities and tensions inherent in the making and implementation of the NCPE (see for example, Evans and Penney 1995; Penney and Evans 1999) and, in the light of these, to address the possibilities for future developments in teaching and learning in physical education. In our discussions here we seek to focus on those possibilities. At the same time, however, we stress that in considering possibilities we should not deny the complexities of policy and curriculum development in physical education, or the tensions that continue to feature in them. We point, therefore, to possibilities within what many may regard as constraining contexts of implementation.

In considering future implementation of the NCPE in primary schools, we also stress that we are not merely concerned with key factors that may make it work. Rather, we wish to move towards a focus upon what teachers want to and can achieve in implementation, and upon what it takes to develop for primary schools an NCPE that expresses inclusivity and equity in physical education, such that it will represent a quality educational experience for *all* pupils. In this chapter we therefore focus upon a number of issues arising in and from the NCPE that can be related to this quest for improved quality and greater equity in physical education, and that link with wider agendas in education, in particular with notions of lifelong learning and preparation for adult life. We acknowledge some critical tensions in our discussions, for on the one hand we identify the NCPE as a restrictive frame imposed upon the subject in conditions of pressure and constraint and, on the other, present it as an increasingly flexible framework within which there is scope for notable developments in teaching and learning in physical education. However, we emphasize that with further revision of the NCPE currently underway (see below), it is time once again to stress the centrality of teachers in determining the nature and quality of the NCPE experienced by children in schools and to focus attention upon exploring opportunities presented by that centrality. We therefore point to the need for a proactive approach in implementation if we are to develop a subject and curricula that make a positive contribution to the education of children facing life in ever-changing and challenging societies.

Finally, it is appropriate for us to acknowledge that we do not claim to research policy and practice in physical education from a position of neutrality. To the contrary, as the preceding discussion indicates, we do so with particular hopes and ambitions for the future development of physical education as a subject in primary and secondary schools, while also accepting that insights from research will only ever be one (and often a marginal) consideration in policy and curriculum development (see for example, Halpin 1994).

The NCPE: An Ever-Changing Scene

Primary teachers, even more than their secondary colleagues, will be aware that the 1990s have been characterized by relentless and exhausting changes to the National Curriculum, driven by successive central governments and their agencies. The National Curriculum, specifically the NCPE, has resulted in a plethora of new documentation and new requirements for school curricula. Implementation of the 1992 order was barely underway before teachers were confronted with the prospect of revised requirements as central government sought to establish a more manageable whole National Curriculum.[1] When the 1995 revisions were acknowledged to have failed to adequately alleviate pressures in primary school curricula, further interim changes were introduced in 1998. It was announced that from September 1998 primary schools would no longer be required to teach the full programmes of study in six national curriculum foundation subjects, which included physical education (Qualifications and Curriculum Authority (QCA) 1998: 3). The only element of the NCPE to remain a statutory requirement was coverage of the programmes of study for swimming.[2] Thus, the NCPE for the primary years has been, and continues to be, the subject of change. Attention is currently directed towards the production of new orders for all curriculum subjects, to be implemented in September 2000. Unsurprisingly, many teachers have felt deeply frustrated both by the pace and the range of demands made of them, and alienated from a policy process that has accorded them little involvement in policy making but required them to shoulder responsibility for whole-scale curriculum development and accept the blame for claimed inadequacies in educational standards (Penney and Evans 1999).

Here we cannot address the detail of all of the above developments, but instead focus upon a number of issues that have emerged throughout the ongoing implementation of the NCPE and that remain pertinent in relation to future implementation. Amidst contexts of rapid and rushed policy development, we are aware that it may be helpful to establish agendas that can endure contexts of rapid social and educational change.

Statutory But Still Low Status

Establishing the provision of physical education as the statutory entitlement for all children was invaluable and something of a landmark in the contemporary history of physical education in England and Wales. Physical education has always been a subject struggling for recognition and resources (particularly timetable time) in schools. To be identified as a foundation subject, a statutory element of the 5–16 curriculum, seemed to signal a new status and security for physical education.[3] Our research and subsequent policy developments, however, have demonstrated that legislative measures offer no guarantee of certainty, and the subject has remained in a somewhat fragile position. Although statutory status may have represented a significant step forward, it is only one small step towards the provision of a quality physical education for *all* pupils in state schools.

Certainly, we would emphasize that physical education's statutory status has to now be regarded as a position of strength from which to move forward, and the indications are that the forthcoming revision of the national curriculum will once again clearly endorse this statutory position. Nevertheless, in contemplating the way forward, we also have to acknowledge that factors other than statutory status may continue to undermine the position of, and prospects for, physical education. In this respect we draw particular attention to the likelihood of continued congestion in the primary school timetable (in view of the emphasis central government has placed on teaching literacy and numeracy), ongoing competition for scarce timetable time, and gross inadequacies in initial teacher training and in-service professional development for teachers (see below).

In considering the position of physical education in the curriculum, it is also timely to draw attention to another long-standing characteristic of life in primary schools: the frequent labelling of physical education as not only marginal to, but also as qualitatively *different* from other aspects of the curriculum, such that it invariably stands alone. In our view, unless tendencies towards isolation and insulation are seriously addressed and a search is made for linkages between teaching and learning in physical education and in other areas of the curriculum, the potential of physical education to be a major contributor to learning across the curriculum will remain regrettably unrealized. We also stress the need for developments that focus upon the links between teaching and learning in physical education and pupils' lives beyond schools. Education as a whole is facing the challenge of establishing greater relevance and coherence in the curriculum, and in the context of physical education, debates on such matters will raise critical questions regarding the future direction, development and implementation of the NCPE. In particular, we emphasize once again the importance of developing curricula that are inclusive, and which enable *all* children to continue involvement in physical activity and/or sport (if they so chose), rather than this being the prerogative of only an able few. Motor elitism remains perhaps the most pervasive (and invidious) but least acknowledged area of inequity in physical education. Revisiting the aims of the subject may be a useful starting point for the development of an inclusive NCPE that has a central role to play in pupils' physical, psychological and social development.

Aims and Expectations

Variously, the official texts of the NCPE have sought to clarify the aims and expectations for teaching and learning in physical education in all state schools. General requirements (featuring in both the 1992 and 1995 orders) together with end of key stage statements (Department of Education and Science (DES) 1992) and subsequently, end of key stage descriptions (Department for Education (DfE) 1995) can be seen as reference points for teachers in this respect. Such texts purport to recognize the diversity of learning that can be nurtured in physical education. They embrace not only the physical aspects of pupils' development, but also the psychological and sociological aspects of participation and performance in physical activity and sport, including attitudes towards physical activity, sport and lifestyles, the development of inter-personal skills and safe practice in the contexts of physical activity and sport. Although laudable, many teachers have questioned how realistic the multiple aims of the NCPE have been, especially when grounded in contexts offering little (resource) support for their implementation (Evans et al. 1996; Evans and Penney 1994). There are also other, important, questions which have remained largely absent from debates accompanying the development and implementation of the NCPE. For example, are the aims of the NCPE adequate and appropriate *educationally*, as well as in relation to more pragmatic concerns? How are these aims reflected in the curricula, teaching and learning of physical education? Furthermore, does the NCPE provide a structural framework that facilitates the realization of these aims?

In the next section we focus on the latter issues, as we reflect upon the degree to which the framework of the NCPE can be regarded as either supporting or inhibiting the development of quality teaching and learning in physical education, the constraints it poses and the possibilities it presents.

Defining the Subject: Directing Teaching and Learning

It was always recognized that designing a National Curriculum for Physical

Education would be far from easy. The subject and the subject community is openly diverse in terms of the interests it represents and variously seeks to promote. In such circumstances, establishing a definition of physical education agreeable to all is problematic and will inevitably privilege some interests at the expense of others. From the outset of the development of the NCPE, physical educationalists were at pains to identify the subject as qualitatively distinct from sport. The non-statutory guidance accompanying the 1992 order sought to clarify and highlight that:

> In *physical education* the emphasis is on learning in a mainly physical context. The purpose of the learning is to develop specific knowledge, skills and understanding and to promote physical development and competence. The learning promotes participation in sport.
>
> (DES 1992, H1, original emphasis)

while:

> *Sport* is the term applied to a range of physical activities where emphasis is on participation and competition. Different sporting activities can and do contribute to learning.
>
> (ibid., original emphasis)

As we have reflected elsewhere (Penney 1999), ironically the long established pattern of curriculum organization in physical education provision, especially in secondary schools, fails to present the subject as anything more than a collection of discrete activities. Largely for political and pragmatic reasons, the NCPE adopted and legitimated this model for physical education in schools, and not only secondary schools. Discrete *areas of activity* were firmly established as the critical reference point in determining breadth and balance in the curriculum (see also Evans and Penney 1995; Penney and Evans 1999).

In the 1992 order, the emphasis was openly towards *increasing* the breadth of coverage in physical education in these terms and thereby extending the range of learning experiences provided for pupils. It was stipulated that the curriculum in key stage 1 (from the start of compulsory education to age 7 years) should encompass programmes of study for five areas of activity (athletic activities, dance, games, gymnastic activities, outdoor and adventurous activities) and, if desired, swimming; while in Key Stage 2 (for ages 7–11 years), the requirement was to pursue all six areas, unless the programme of study for swimming had been completed in Key Stage 1 (DES 1992). Since 1992 the revisions to the requirements for NCPE have centred upon *reducing* the statutory coverage of areas of activity and establishing a privileged status for games within the activity-based framework (see Evans and Penney 1995; Penney and Evans 1997, 1999). In relation to Key Stages 1 and 2, requirements and advice can be seen as moving back towards a focus upon the provision of games, dance and gymnastics, together with swimming at Key Stage 2. In 1995 coverage of games, gymnastics and dance was established as the focus for Key Stage 1, with the option to also follow the Key Stage 2 programme of study for swimming, while, for Key Stage 2, a requirement to address all areas remained in place, but with priorities clearly emerging. It was stated:

> During *each year* of the key stage pupils should be taught Games, Gymnastics Activities and Dance. At *points during* the key stage pupils should be taught Athletic Activities, Outdoor and Adventurous Activities, and Swimming unless they have already completed the programme of study for Swimming in Key Stage 1.
>
> (DfE/WO 1995: **4**, our emphasis)

These revisions appeared to signal significant improvements in terms of the manageability of the NCPE at Key Stage 1, but did little to reduce the perceived overload at Key Stage 2. In 1998 the Office of Her Majesty's Chief Inspector of Schools in Wales (OHMCI) reported that in Key Stage 1 'time is generally sufficient to offer pupils a broad and balanced range of experiences', but that in Key Stage 2 'schools are often hard pressed to meet all the requirements of the NC in the time allocated' (OHCMI 1998: 16).

As indicated above, the next move (in 1998) was to a situation in which only the programmes of study for swimming were statutory. Notably, this announcement was accompanied by guidance designed to ensure retention of some notion of breadth and balance in physical education. Specifically, schools were advised to retain games, dance and gymnastics activities in Key Stage 1 (QCA 1998). With respect to Key Stage 2, they faced the somewhat contradictory advice on the one hand to 'Retain the six areas of activity, but give priority to some areas. For instance, *teach swimming and give priority to the teaching of dance, games and gymnastic activities*' (ibid.: 19, original emphasis), and on the other to 'Teach fewer areas of activity. For instance, *omit outdoor and adventurous activities*' (ibid.: 19, original emphasis). In 2000, it seems likely that primary schools will once again face a statutory requirement to follow programmes of study for games, dance and gymnastics activities in Key Stage 1, with the option of also following a new programme of study for swimming activities and water safety in Key Stage 1, and in Key Stage 2, to follow programmes of study for five areas of activity, comprising dance activities, games activities, gymnastic activities and two other areas from swimming and water safety, athletic activities, and outdoor and adventurous activities (with swimming and water safety statutory unless pupils have completed the full programme of study for this area of activity in Key Stage 1) (QCA 1999).

A Flawed Framework?

Most notably, this area of activity framework appeared to impose a 'secondary' and distinctly 'specialist' frame upon physical education in the primary curriculum. Particularly at Key Stage 2, the requirements could be regarded as a move away from more holistic programmes centring on the development of 'movement skills' (see also Jones 1996) and to have encouraged curricular divisions rather than linkages in teaching and learning. The recently published Office for Standards in Education (Ofsted) report relating to initial teacher training in primary physical education, highlights the degree to which the NCPE has reinforced divisions within the subject. It is stated that 'Most primary trainees see the subject as comprising separate groups of activities – games, dance, gymnastics, athletics, OAA and swimming.[4] They are not secure in their understanding of the nature of the subject as a whole, or of what is to be learned, other than to produce performers of particular activities' (Ofsted 1998: 5). It is not surprising that the requirement to follow programmes of study in multiple areas, each emphasized as distinct, has not only added to many teachers' feelings of inadequacy in terms of their ability to teach physical education, but also fragmented and diminished the focus of the learning experience. Both issues are highlighted by Dunn, who comments that

> The National Curriculum has not, in my opinion, enhanced the quality of teaching in Primary Schools. It has consisted of a list of activities which schools could aim to provide, in many cases with limited success. The six areas of PE at KS2 and three at KS1 have left some colleagues floundering.
>
> (1998: 13)

The NCPE's framework can thus be seen as prompting a focus upon skills, knowledge and understanding that are *specific to the activity* (or sport) context, over and above an emphasis upon teaching and learning associated with common themes and broader educational agendas and goals. There seems an inherent danger of diminishing, or perhaps losing sight of altogether, the 'education' in physical education. Once again, the recent Ofsted report makes some relevant observations. The report states that the 'lack of deep understanding of the nature of the subject and of its purpose in the National Curriculum often leads to fragmentation and a lack of progression in trainees' planning for teaching and learning. Each activity, even each game, is all too easily seen as an area of learning in its own right, with no consideration of how elements in the different areas of work are complementary' (1998: 5).

In looking to the future, therefore, we need to again ask what we are aiming to achieve in and through physical education, and then question whether or not the NCPE (its programmes of study and the curricula derived from them), adequately support the realization of those aims. In our view, the organizational framework for the NCPE does little to further an understanding (either within or beyond the profession) that the subject 'uses many of the same activities as sport and leisure, *but for a different purpose*, and with *different* teaching methods and priorities in terms of learning outcomes' (Williams 1989: 16, our emphasis). The forthcoming revision of the NCPE may, however, provide greater clarity for teachers in relation to physical education's purposes and priorities in learning outcomes. We anticipate that the new requirements (to be implemented in September 2000) will endorse the 'core strands of learning' identified in draft proposals (QCA 1999) and currently labelled as:

- Acquiring and developing skills
- Selecting and applying
- Evaluating and improving performance
- Knowledge and understanding of health and fitness.

(QCA 1999: 171)

Establishing these strands is intended to provide a clearer focus for teaching and learning (see Casbon 1999). This restructuring can be seen as an attempt to give a more central position to issues previously addressed in the 'general requirements' for the subject (DES 1992; DfE/WO 1995), and thereby *ensure* that they are clearly reflected in teaching and learning. Focusing upon strands may indeed help to reduce gaps and unnecessary overlap in pupils' learning experiences, and draw attention to the fact that, for example, 'Some areas such as games offer a wide range of potential activities yet may provide very similar learning experiences' (Curriculum Council for Wales (CCW) 1994: 6). This is a matter that needs to be addressed across all areas of activity, and not only within any one.

However, there remains an apparent tension in the proposed new framework for the NCPE, in that the creation of strands looks set to be accompanied by the continued definition of 'breadth of study' as coverage of 'areas of activity' (rather than coverage of the strands) and the retention of programmes of study centring upon areas of activity (rather than strands). Teachers, therefore, will face new challenges when implementing the NCPE: to achieve progression in learning associated with the strands while implementing programmes of study that relate to areas of activity. This will not be an easy task (particularly when they also face new demands and challenges in other areas of the primary curriculum and when advisory support and/or professional development opportunities relating to physical education are invariably lacking; see Evans and Penney 1994). Notwithstanding these difficulties, our hope is that primary teachers will welcome this characteristic of the new NCPE, and take the lead in establishing greater coherency within physical education and between it and other aspects of the curriculum (see also Piotrowski in Chapter 4).

Planning, Performing and Evaluating

Another prominent characteristic of the NCPE has been the identification of planning, performing and evaluating as three inter-related elements of physical education, to be addressed throughout teaching; in curriculum planning, lesson design and assessment in physical education. This emphasis on educational processes (rather than mechanical practices and outcomes) in physical education was a matter of tension in the development of the NCPE. Conservative politicians in particular, needed 'reassurance' that the subject would remain essentially active in nature and maintain an interest in performance outcomes as well as process (Evans and Penney 1995; Penney and Evans 1999). Thus, NCPE texts have repeatedly emphasized that the 'performance' aspect should remain the focus of attention. Most recently teachers were advised to 'place the greatest emphasis on performance' in their Key Stage 1 curriculum (QCA 1998). While 'planning, performing and evaluating' may now be familiar terminology in primary physical education, it is clear that in both primary and secondary schools, facilitating progression in learning that relates to planning and evaluation, within an active teaching context, remains an aspect of implementation in which further support is needed.

As well as pointing to the difficulties of achieving the integration of planning, performing and evaluating in teaching and learning, debates about these matters demand that we again revisit the aims and purposes of physical education. In our view, although 'being active' is an important characteristic of physical education, attention also needs to be directed towards the learning experiences that 'being active' is facilitating. While it may be realistic and highly appropriate to identify physical education as having a key role to play in the development of attitudes and behaviours that characterize active and healthy lives, it would be inappropriate and unrealistic for physical education to be regarded as the arena to bring about immediate improvements in pupils' physical health. This would be to reduce physical education to physical fitness or training (a profoundly retrograde step) or, worse still, to the antics of a red-coat entertainer, managing a subject that 'is about "letting off steam" and is fundamentally "recreational" rather than "educational"' (Shaughnessy and Price 1995: 37).

If teachers and teacher educators are to develop physical education curricula that express and promote greater inclusivity, a far broader conceptualization of performance will need to be developed and adopted. Currently there is a tendency for performance to be associated primarily, if not exclusively, with elite performance in specific sports. Such a focus is in danger of directing teaching and learning in physical education towards only one narrow arena of application that will ultimately be relevant to very few pupils. Our hope is that the ongoing implementation of the NCPE, and particularly the new order, will encourage teachers to recognize that performance in sport can take many forms and occur in many contexts, and be an enjoyable pursuit for people of all abilities. Unless physical education curricula, teaching and learning express and promote this diversity, we are unlikely to succeed in providing all pupils with opportunities to experience enjoyment and achievement in contexts of physical activity and sport. While this is undoubtedly a matter for both secondary and primary teachers, the significance of early experiences in primary schools in shaping future interests and involvement, cannot be underestimated. Regrettably the importance of the subject in primary schools is not reflected in the provision of training, resources or support. As we discuss in the next section, curriculum design, teaching and learning in physical education all remain severely constrained by these matters (see also Evans et al. 1996).

Pragmatics in Practice

We are all too aware that the issues discussed above are not the only factors shaping the implementation of the NCPE, or those most immediately recognizable as determining the quality of pupils' experiences in physical education. Aspects of resourcing of physical education (specifically, timetabling allocations and arrangements, staff expertise and confidence, facilities, funding and equipment and, overlying all of these, the views and decisions of headteachers in primary schools), are all far more obvious influences on these experiences. The picture of the NCPE to emerge from our research is not one of homogeneity and equity in provision but rather of difference, contingent upon the relative 'poverty' or 'wealth' of contexts of schooling, and thus of considerable variation in the statutory entitlement experienced by children in different schools (see Evans et al. 1996). Throughout our research we have highlighted that the 'flexibility' inherent in the NCPE has allowed for these differences to remain a feature of implementation, and recent inspection reports confirm the continued pattern of resource-driven planning and provision in physical education. For example, in Wales it has been reported that deficiencies in accommodation (physical plant) and resources continue to 'adversely affect the quality of educational provision and standards of pupils' achievements in many primary schools' and that 'The difficulties tend to be most acute in small schools' (OHMCI 1998: 3). More specifically it is reported that while there have been significant improvements in standards in Key Stage 2 physical education in 1996–7, 'Relatively few schools achieve consistently good standards across the full range of activities prescribed by the NC', that 'there are continuing weaknesses in key aspects of the work in physical education in around 55% of primary', and that 'The overall quality of teaching continues to improve, but can vary widely within individual schools' (ibid.: 2).

Looking ahead to the implementation of the new orders in 2000, we can expect pragmatic matters to remain a key concern for primary schools. The proposed reinstatement of statutory requirement to cover multiple areas of activity (see above) seem hardly likely to reduce these concerns (and particularly those relating to the expertise required of teachers to 'deliver' the NCPE, given continued inadequacies in both initial and in-service training for primary teachers). As emphasized above, the evidence from recent Ofsted inspections confirms that investment in training fails to come anywhere close to the importance sometimes associated with teaching and learning in physical education during the primary years in the rhetoric of political debate (see Ofsted 1998).

However, while acknowledging that resource concerns are important issues in and of themselves, we also draw attention to the connections between these and other matters discussed earlier: specifically, how expertise is defined, and the isolation and low status of physical education in the curriculum. Revisiting the purposes and focus of the subject, restructuring curricula accordingly and refocusing teaching and learning, could, we suggest, help reduce some of the constraints on the implementation of the NCPE. At the same time we are aware that repeated change is rarely, if ever, going to be considered popular or realistic in the perspectives of overworked and under-resourced teachers, many of whom feel that they are already struggling to stand still and survive. Thus, reassuringly, in the current revision there has been an open commitment to avoiding 'excessive disruption and upheaval in the curriculum' (Gilliver 1999: 5). Whilst this is welcome recognition of the constraints under which teachers work it will also pose a real dilemma and challenge for them; either to accommodate the new requirements within largely unchanged practice, or to look to re-shape curricula, teaching and learning in new and innovative ways. Below we expand upon some of the issues associated with the latter and stress in particular that pursuing these opportunities will need to be a collaborative endeavour involving many agencies and individuals if innovation is to be successful and enduring.

Possibilities and Partnerships

First and foremost, we emphasize the need for curriculum developments to be undertaken in *partnership with pupils*. Their involvement in curriculum planning, the identification of learning objectives, the design of learning experiences that will facilitate the achievement of these, and in assessment, will be critical if the aspiration is to achieve greater inclusivity, and to provide all pupils with a sense of ownership of knowledge of, and purpose in, physical education. These matters also need to be addressed in training institutions particularly in the light of reports that 'very few trainees are successful in enabling pupils to reflect, refine, interpret and adapt personal responses to ensure a good match to the purpose of the task' (Ofsted 1998: 7).

Next, any endeavour to raise (and change) expectations relating to learning in physical education will need to be approached in *partnership with parents*. Understandably, many parents, like politicians, may have little appreciation of the educational aims and expectations of physical education, but rather may see its focus as the attainment of (only) skills and competencies in specific sports. This may be a view shared by many teachers in primary schools. The future implementation of the NCPE must therefore actively involve *all staff*, and particularly *headteachers*, if a broader view of physical education and its purposes is to be cultivated. A collaborative approach to implementation will be vital if links are to be made between physical education and other areas of the primary curriculum, and if its potential contribution to the overall education of the child is to materialize.

Much of our discussion to date has also pointed to the critical role that *higher education and initial teacher training* has to play in shaping future teaching of physical education in primary schools. The quality of training now relies very heavily on the quality of partnerships inherent in training, in particular, between training institutions and schools, and between schools and their trainees. A recent Ofsted (1998) report emphasized that training tutors, mentors and headteachers are all key figures influencing the quality of the trainee's experience, as is communication between them. Unfortunately the report also identifies that support for teaching physical education, together with other foundation subjects, is invariably lacking in primary training. Inadequacies have then been exacerbated by the demise in recent years of another key partnership in education, between teachers and *Local Education Authority* (LEA) advisors (see Evans and Penney 1994). Regrettably, the decline of the LEAs, which has made collaboration across schools more difficult, has coincided with a period when working together and sharing ideas has become even more important for many teachers. Communication with *colleagues in other schools*, and the maintenance of clusters of schools remain essential elements of support in implementation of policy and in curriculum development. They are also mechanisms that are clearly very fragile in contexts of restricted funding for professional development, particularly in non-core subjects such as physical education (Evans et al. 1996; Shaughnessy and Price 1995).

Colleagues in *secondary schools* are not only a potential source of advice and support for primary teachers, but also a vital link if we are to see greater continuity and coherency in teaching and learning in physical education across key stages. In these respects implementation of the NCPE has been notably lacking to date and links across sectors are likely to become even more important in the future, with the prospect of greater diversity in the experiences of pupils entering Key Stage 3 than is currently the case. While it may be hoped that a newly created eight-level scale of attainment in physical education (see QCA 1999) will provide an invaluable tool for improved planning for progression in teaching and learning, levels are unlikely either to be effective or operational unless there is collaboration between primary and secondary teachers.

In these difficult contexts of implementation the support for physical education that has come from 'outside' the profession, and in particular, from the *Youth Sport Trust* (YST) (a privately funded, charitable body) is to be especially welcomed. The resources and associated training developed by the YST have proved invaluable for many teachers faced with the task of implementing the NCPE with limited resources and this partnership, amongst others, will need to be pursued. However (as the YST themselves stress: see for example YST 1996), their resources do not constitute a curriculum, nor is their training regarded as an adequate replacement for comprehensive initial and in-service training in physical education. In approaching implementation, YST materials and other packages produced for example by national governing bodies can, if used selectively, provide invaluable support for implementation, but they do not constitute implementation of the NCPE. Similarly, other individuals, such as sports development officers, may also have an important part to play in implementation, *if* their agendas are in harmony with the interests of inclusivity and aims of the NCPE. OHMCI's report that activities provided by sports development officers 'are not always well-matched to the requirements of the NC nor are they always appropriate to pupils' stage of development and current learning needs' (1998: 14) reinforces the need for a retention of the centrality of educational aims and of teachers in the implementation of the NCPE. In considering partnerships, we also again stress the need for diversity in provision. Well planned partnerships, facilitating linkages to a *variety* of arenas of sport and recreation, may well be a precursor to offering more pupils (not only a few) choices and abilities to participate in physical recreation and to achieve active and healthy lives.

Conclusion

Perhaps above all other characteristics of the NCPE, its flexibility will need attention if an inclusive and equitable physical education curriculum is to be achieved. Throughout the implementation of the NCPE, we have seen that its requirements have permitted creativity in curriculum design, teaching and learning, but have also nurtured diversity in practice, advantaging some children and disadvantaging others in their experiences of physical education. Flexibility in statutory requirements is inevitably janus-headed; potentially a basis for progressive development, or for a minimalistic response to 'new' requirements that thereby may merely act to maintain an inadequate status quo (Penney and Evans 1999). The move towards the next phase of implementation of the NCPE may do little to alter this inequitable state of affairs. At the time of the last revision of the NCPE we suggested that the new order 'may act as an impetus for schools to begin or make further progress towards curriculum development in physical education. Alternatively, its text may merely reinforce the apparent absence of curriculum change' (Penney and Evans 1999: 39). In this respect the current revision of the NCPE, perhaps to a greater extent than previous NCPE texts, poses a real dilemma and challenge for physical education teachers and teacher trainers: whether to retain the status quo, or seek to take the subject in new directions. In 1996 the 'picture' our research painted of the NCPE in primary schools was of practices that were 'unfinished, unclear and not altogether rosy' (Evans et al. 1996: 38). Will the new orders foster progress? It remains to be seen. Once again we are addressing a changing scene and we stand on the edge of an opportunity, either for progressive development, or surface level change.

Acknowledgement

The support of the Leverhulme Trust in funding research drawn upon in this chapter is greatly appreciated (1994–1996; project reference No. F1800).

Notes

1   The term 'order' denotes the statutory status of requirements.
2   'Programmes of study' refers to the matters, skills and processes which must be taught to pupils in order for them to meet the objectives set out in attainment targets for subjects.
3   The Education Reform Act 1988 identified 'core' (English, mathematics, science and in Welsh speaking schools in Wales, Welsh) and 'foundation' (technology, history, geography, music, art, physical education, modern foreign languages, and in non-Welsh speaking schools in Wales, Welsh) subjects for the National Curriculum.
4   OAA is an abbreviation for 'Outdoor and Adventurous Activities'.

References

Casbon, C. (1999) 'National curriculum review – key points in the review of the order', *British Journal of Physical Education* 30,1, 6–7.

Curriculum Council for Wales (1994) *A Curriculum Leader's Guide to Physical Education in the National Curriculum at KS1 and KS2.* Cardiff: CCW.

DES (1992) *Physical Education in the National Curriculum.* London: DES.

DfE (1995) *Physical Education in the National Curriculum.* London: DfE.

Dunn, A. (1998) 'Quality not quantity will have a positive effect on P.E. in primary schools', *Primary PE Focus* Autumn, 13–14.

Evans, J. and Penney, D. (1994) 'Whatever happened to good advice? Service and inspection after the Education Reform Act, *British Educational Research Journal* 20, 5, 519–33.

—— (1995) 'Physical education, restoration and the politics of sport, *Curriculum Studies* 3, 2, 183–96.

Evans, J. and Penney, D. with Bryant, A. and Hennink, M. (1996) 'All things bright and beautiful? PE in primary schools post the 1988 ERA', *Educational Review* 48, 1, 29–40.

Gilliver, K. (1999) 'Physical education 2000: review of the national curriculum, *British Journal of Physical Education* 30, 1, 4–5.

Halpin, D. (1994) 'Practice and prospects in education policy research', in D. Halpin and B. Troyna (eds) *Researching Education Policy: Ethical and methodological issues.* London: Falmer Press.

Jones, C. (1996) 'Physical education at Key Stage 1', in N. Armstrong (ed.) *New Directions in Physical Education.* London: Cassell.

Ofsted (1998) *Teaching Physical Education in the Primary School: The initial training of teachers.* Ofsted.

OHMCI (1998) *Standards and Quality in Primary Schools: Physical education and sport.* Cardiff: OHMCI.

Penney, D. (1999) 'New agendas for the new millennium?' Paper presented at the PEAUK Centenary Conference, University of Bath, 19–20 April 1999.

Penney, D. and Evans, J. (1997) 'Naming the game: discourse and domination in physical education and sport in England and Wales', *European Physical Education Review* 3, 1, 21–32.

—— (1999) *Politics, Policy and Practice in Physical Education*. London: Routledge.

QCA (1998) *Maintaining Breadth and Balance at Key Stages 1 and 2*. London: QCA.

—— (1999) *The Review of the National Curriculum in England: The consultation materials*. London: QCA.

Shaughnessy, J. and Price, L. (1995) 'Physical education in primary schools: what's been going on since September 1992?', *The Bulletin of Physical Education* 31, 2, 34–42.

Williams, A. (1989) 'The place of physical education in primary education', in A. Williams (ed.) *Issues in Physical Education for the Primary Years*. London: Falmer Press.

Youth Sport Trust (YST) (1996) 'TOP Opportunities for Primary Schools', *Primary PE Focus* Spring, 11–14.

3   Couch Potato Kids and Lazy Layabouts

The Role of Primary Schools in Relation to Physical Activity Among Children

Mike Sleap, Peter Warburton and Michael Waring

These words are typical of newspaper headlines that seek to sensationalize the apparent lack of physical activity undertaken by children today. In a more reserved tone, similar concerns have been expressed in the academic world by researchers such as Armstrong: 'Sustained periods of physical activity are not characteristic of children's physical activity patterns.... The challenge to physical education and sport is to promote and foster active lifestyles which are likely to be sustained into adult life' (1998: 8).

This chapter aims to explore whether children are inactive and whether there are implications in terms of maintaining good health. Following this discussion, there will be consideration of the role of primary schools in relation to physical activity among children. The chapter will be divided into the following sections:

- A brief exploration of the relationship between physical activity and health;
- Issues concerning the assessment of children's physical activity levels;
- Current knowledge about children's physical activity levels;
- The role of the primary school in promoting active lifestyles among children;
- Concluding comments.

First, however, it is necessary to clarify the main terms that will be used in the chapter. The focus will be on children of primary school age and this means that the discussion will be concerned with pre-pubescent young people. It is important to note that any reference to physical activity will include physically active sport (for example, swimming), functional activities (for example, cycling to school) and play activities (for example, skipping). Finally, it should be recognized that, while the term health is often viewed broadly as psychological, social and physical well-being, research concerned with physical activity and health concentrates mainly on the physical dimension and reducing the risk of disease.

A Brief Exploration of the Relationship between Physical Activity and Health

While a physically active lifestyle can offer many benefits to human beings, its role in contributing to health has been a topic of interest in recent years and is the main theme of this chapter. In modern Britain it is possible to lead a relatively sedentary life, an active life or one which lies somewhere in between. It is of some significance, therefore, to find that, when all other things are equal, adults who lead active lives have a substantially reduced risk of suffering many life-threatening diseases, and especially cardiovascular diseases (Riddoch 1998). While it would be useful to have an accepted, precise definition of the level of physical activity needed to stay healthy, the complexity of the issue prevents a neat answer. Nevertheless, current thinking indicates that regular (daily or nearly every day), sustained (15 to 30 minutes), moderate intensity physical activity (comparable to brisk walking) offers the best kind of health benefits for adults (Bouchard et al. 1994).

These criteria reflect a shift in attitude in recent years. Extensive analysis of epidemiological studies (for example, Blair 1993) has led to a re-assessment of the necessity for vigorous exercise to lower the risk of cardiovascular disease, originally proposed by Morris and others (Morris et al. 1980; Paffenbarger et al. 1978). It would appear that moderate intensity physical activity offers the best protection against health problems and current recommendations reflect this. Another development relates to the duration of physical activity sessions. On this issue there is growing acceptance that short bouts of physical activity of perhaps 10 to 15 minutes can be as valuable as longer, continuous periods (DeBusk et al. 1990; Haskell 1994).

For children the relationship between physical activity and health is different. At the present time, research suggests that children do not seem to suffer from poor health as a consequence of inactive lifestyles. Many studies show no association between children's physical activity levels and particular health parameters, while others show only a weak association at best (Riddoch 1998). The reasons for this may be:

- Assessments of children's physical activity are lacking in accuracy;
- Weakness in the design of research studies – for example, studies are too short to produce effects;
- Despite media hype, children are sufficiently active to maintain reasonable health.

While the above considerations may help to explain the situation, it is also true that most health problems emerge in middle or old age and it is not surprising that there is little change in risk factors during childhood. In other words, there has not been enough time for health problems to develop to the extent that they can be ameliorated by physical activity interventions.

Is it the case, therefore, that there is no serious problem and, consequently, little point in attempting to increase physical activity levels among children? In order to answer this question, it is necessary to look closer at research conducted to assess children's physical activity levels.

Issues Concerning the Assessment of Children's Physical Activity Levels

Cale (1998) identified more than thirty different procedures for assessing physical activity, but acknowledged that there were only a limited number appropriate for use with young people. The Health Education Authority (HEA) has also stated that 'the accurate measurement and assessment of physical activity tends to be problematic in terms of definition, reliability and validity' (Health Education Authority 1997: 66).

Self-report measures, such as questionnaires and diary accounts, are relatively easy to administer and allow for large numbers to be assessed. However, their accuracy has often been called into question, especially in relation to children's ability to recall behaviour and a tendency for them to overestimate physical activity levels (Telema et al. 1985; Baranowski 1988). Observational methods, where researchers observe a child's physical activity behaviour, offer greater accuracy about physical activity levels and, additionally, can identify the type of activity undertaken. However, because of high cost implications, they cannot be utilized with large numbers of children.

Physiological measurement devices, such as heart rate monitors, can be worn by children to assess relative duration and intensity of physical activity. Intervening factors such as emotional state, temperature, humidity, fatigue and state of hydration can influence heart rate measurements and, again, cost implications restrict the number of children that can be assessed. Motion sensors, such as accelerometers, are mechanical devices which can be attached to individuals to estimate physical activity levels. In addition to some of the limitations mentioned above, such as cost implications for large samples, motion sensors often only measure certain types of movement and their accuracy is questionable (Health Education Authority 1997).

Current Knowledge about Children's Physical Activity Levels

The difficulties of assessing children's physical activity levels are compounded by the issue of making meaningful interpretations of research findings. The problems can be grouped into three areas. First, many studies have focused on specific aspects of children's lives, for example time at school, which means that their findings only offer a partial view of children's lifestyles. This limitation is further pronounced if assessments are conducted at certain times of the year, thus omitting the variability in physical activity behaviour caused by seasonal activities and, of course, the British weather. Second, very few studies have used a combination of methods to corroborate findings. Studies using heart rate monitoring, direct observation and motion sensors provide detailed evidence but on very small samples which can in no way be considered representative of British children. On the other hand, studies utilizing self-report methods have limited accuracy, as mentioned earlier, and very few have been conducted with children under 10 years of age.

Finally, because of unclear definitions of health-promoting physical activity, authors have discussed their results according to different physical activity criteria, making comparisons across studies very difficult. For example, many research studies of children's physical activity levels have been analysed in terms of recommended levels of physical activity for adults. This may have been misleading, especially because the criterion of 20 minutes' sustained physical activity is not a natural feature of children's behaviour. The situation should now improve because the HEA has published the following recommendations for young people and physical activity, based on current scientific evidence and expert opinion.

Recommendations for Young People and Physical Activity

Primary recommendations

- All young people should participate in physical activity of at least moderate intensity for *one hour per day*.
- Young people who currently do little activity should participate in physical activity of at least moderate intensity for *at least half an hour per day*.

Secondary recommendation

- *At least twice a week*, some of these activities should help to enhance and maintain muscular strength and flexibility and bone health (HEA 1998: 3).

Moderate intensity physical activity is defined as 'activity usually equivalent to brisk walking, which might be expected to leave the participant feeling warm and slightly out of breath' (HEA 1998: 2). An important ancillary point is the recommendation that physical activity can be undertaken either continuously or *accumulated intermittently during the day*. Thus, research studies also need to be analysed in terms of this consideration.

The first point to be made is that relatively few research studies have examined the physical activity levels of primary school age children in the UK. A number have been conducted in other countries (for example, Baranowski et al. 1987; Bailey et al. 1995) but, because of cultural differences, their findings cannot easily be applied to the UK and they will not be considered in this review.

Self-report studies

Most of the studies in the UK using self-report methods have been aimed at adolescents and those including primary age children suffer from many limitations. An example is the study conducted by Thirlaway and Benton (1993) of children in West Glamorgan. First, while the research included both primary and secondary school children, the youngest age group in the survey were 10- and 11-year-olds, thus offering no data on children any younger. Second, while the activity diary method seems to have been administered carefully, the problems associated with this method can be gauged by the fact that it was accepted that all children took part in each physical activity at the same intensity. This is palpably not the case since, in a game like football, a child who plays as goalkeeper, for example, will not expend the same energy as an outfield player. The contention by the authors that leisure time physical activity showed a dramatic decline during the transition from primary to secondary school age may be correct, but the findings cannot offer information about the full age range of primary school children and whether or not they meet the HEA physical activity recommendations.

Using a self-report questionnaire, Shropshire and Carroll concluded that low physical activity levels were evident among 924 10- and 11-year-old children. While their survey involved one of the largest samples of children in the UK, the authors admitted that 'The seven-day recall method adopted in the present study may not have captured the children's true activity patterns or the children may have been wrongly categorised as having satisfied, or not, specific activity recommendations which may be inappropriate for their age' (1998: 164).

Direct observation studies

A series of studies of primary age children was conducted by Sleap and Warburton (1996) using the direct observation method. The advantage of this method is that precise data can be collected regarding the type and level of physical activity undertaken by children, with a points system used to differentiate intensity of physical activity. In total, 179 children aged from 5 to 11 years were observed at different times of the year during school break times, lunch times, physical education lessons and free time outside of school.

One of their conclusions illustrates the variability in interpretation that can emerge from studies such as this: 'Only 38 children (21%) engaged in a sustained 20-min period of moderate to vigorous physical activity (MVPA), but nearly all children (95%) took part in a 5-min period of MVPA' (Sleap and Warburton 1996: 248).

Thus, based on criteria for recommended physical activity levels which require 20 minutes of sustained physical activity, it would seem that most children were insufficiently active. However, if intermittent accumulation of physical activity is accepted, it is possible that nearly all the children in these studies could have met the HEA recommendations. Indeed, the authors estimated that children were engaged in moderate intensity physical activity for an average of 117 minutes per day, almost twice the recommendation of the HEA.

There are two main qualifications that need to be made regarding this apparently encouraging assessment. First, the sample of 179 children is small and can in no way be representative of the UK childhood population; further assessments are necessary to establish whether these kinds of physical activity levels are widespread. Second, a large proportion of the moderate intensity physical activity occurred at school and, since children attend school for little more than half the days in a year, the overall lifestyle of children may be somewhat less active.

Heart rate monitoring

Heart rate monitoring can offer accurate assessments of children's physical activity patterns. However, there have only been a small number of studies carried out in the UK and these have mainly focused on children aged 10 and 11 years of age. Using heart rate data from 332 children, with a mean age of 10.9 years, Armstrong and Welsman (1997) reported that, during 12-hour monitoring periods, about half of the children did not engage in more than one 10-minute sustained period of moderate physical activity equivalent to a brisk walk. Interestingly, if the issue of sustained physical activity is put aside again, the percentage of accumulated, moderate physical activity experienced by these children was 9.2 per cent for boys and 7.7 per cent for girls. This works out at around 66 minutes per day for boys and 55 minutes per day for girls, which fulfils the primary recommendation of the HEA almost exactly.

Once again, there are certain qualifications that need to be made in relation to these findings. The limited number of children assessed means that generalizations need to be cautious and, even then, must be mainly limited to 10- and 11-year-olds and not younger children. There are other problems as well, since no heart rate monitoring studies in the UK have examined physical activity during the summer vacation and little is known about the influence on heart rate of emotional state, temperature and fatigue among children.

Conclusions About Physical Activity Assessments of Children

It must be concluded that there is still much to be investigated with regard to children's physical activity levels. The integrity of findings from self-report assessments is questionable and the numbers of children involved in studies using objective measures are too small to warrant robust generalizations. The evidence in respect of children under 10 years of age is negligible.

Adopting a fair degree of caution, we can say the indications are that some children accumulate an hour per day of moderate intensity physical activity. Nevertheless, there could be many children who fall well short of this criterion.

Also, the accumulation is likely to be made up of relatively short bursts of physical activity, with continuous periods of longer than 5 minutes quite rare.

It is possible that boys are more active than girls, although the bulk of evidence pointing to this comes from assessments of 10- and 11-year-olds. The studies of Sleap and Warburton (1996), while limited to small numbers, showed no difference in physical activity levels among the full range of 5- to 11-year-olds. There would appear to be a sharp decline in physical activity levels between primary school and secondary school children, although there are no figures to show whether there is a decline during the primary school years.

While the above conclusions would seem to be at variance with recent concerns about children's physical activity levels, the authors believe there are persuasive reasons why physical activity should still be promoted among children.

- First, the evidence is certainly not clear about children's physical activity levels. Further research may find that, in whatever way the analysis is performed, children's physical activity levels do not reach recommended levels.
- If it is true that, at present, children's moderate intensity physical activity mainly occurs at school, there needs to be very real concern about children's physical activity behaviour outside of school.
- Without intervention, the lifestyles of children in the future are likely to become more sedentary since transportation systems will continue to improve, passive recreations will become ever more appealing and adult role models will be more and more inactive.
- It has been suggested that active children turn into active adults. While the soundness of this proposition has not been safely proven, there are an increasing number of well constructed studies which point to this kind of tracking principle (Glenmark et al. 1994; Kuh and Cooper 1992).

The Role of the Primary School in Promoting Active Lifestyles among Children

There are many reasons for laying the foundation of a physically active lifestyle at an early age. While the decline in activity levels and the incidence of diseases may emerge from the teenage years and beyond, it is undoubtedly the case that the seeds of these developments are rooted in childhood. Most crucially, it is the way in which an active lifestyle is 'valued' that holds the key to this issue. The child that dislikes maths often grows up to dislike all kinds of mathematical calculations in later life. In the same way, the child who has negative physical activity experiences often grows up to perceive physical activity as something to be avoided.

The need for concerted action to promote active lifestyles among young people has been voiced many times (for example, Armstrong and Welsman

1997; Sleap 1997). The greatest impact will be made if parents, community leaders, doctors, media personalities and teachers all encourage young people to be active. The primary school is a vital ingredient in this comprehensive approach and can make a telling difference, without necessarily adding anything extra to existing teacher workloads.

It is argued here that primary schools can create a powerful impact simply by valuing the notion of an active lifestyle. No money is required, no planning to be done and no paperwork needed – it is simply a matter of developing a school ethos where physical activity is accepted as an enjoyable and all-embracing feature of everyday life. It may be that primary school teachers think that this is something they already do, and yet it involves something different from offering occasional platitudes like 'exercise is good for you' or running successful football and netball teams.

A primary school which expresses a vibrant and inspirational ethos about physical activity might have an exciting environment to stimulate physical activity, both inside and out. For example, displays can illustrate ordinary young people engaged in rewarding activities like skipping, cycling and swimming and not just the sporting idols of the time. All adults in the school, including non-teaching staff, can express positive 'vibes' to children about physical activity by the way they talk and act. Active, adult role models are ideal but, if this is not possible, all adults in the school should always talk about physical activity in a positive way.

While a positive approach to active lifestyles can be achieved through the ethos of the school, there are many other ways open to primary schools. The remainder of the chapter explores both curricular and extended curriculum opportunities to promote physical activity among young people.

Curriculum Opportunities

The promotion of physical activity is not simply limited to curriculum opportunities in the PE lesson. While children may enjoy dance or short tennis in their PE lessons, there will be a longer-term influence if, during classroom lessons, they can be helped to understand why and how an active lifestyle improves the quality of their lives. In recent years, resources from the British Heart Foundation, the Happy Heart Project and Loughborough University have been developed to help primary school teachers educate children about physical activity and the body (details of these are listed at the end of the chapter).

While there has been no investigation of the extent to which this topic area has been included in children's education, there can be some confidence that it is quite widespread, not least because it forms part of the National Curriculum. Schools can address the relationship between physical activity and health throughout Key Stages 1 and 2 in a number of Programmes of Study of the National Curriculum:

Science: Life Processes and Living Things

Key Stage 1   *Pupils should be taught that taking exercise helps humans to keep healthy*

Key Stage 2   *Pupils should be taught the effects of exercise and rest on pulse rate*

(DfE 1995: 40, 45)

Physical Education

Key Stages 1 and 2   *To promote physical activity and healthy lifestyles, pupils should be taught:*

(a) to be physically active;
(b) to adopt the best possible posture and the appropriate use of the body;
(c) to engage in activities that develop cardiovascular health, flexibility, muscular strength and endurance;
(d) the increasing need for personal hygiene in relation to vigorous physical activity.

(DfE 1995: 114)

Health Education

Key Stage 1   *Pupils should know:*

that people feel better when they take regular exercise;
that exercise uses energy which comes from food.

Key Stage 2   *Pupils should know:*

that exercise strengthens bones, muscles and organs and keeps the body supple;
that if energy intake is greater than expenditure of energy, the body stores the excess as fat.

(DfE 1990:12, 14)

For the future, however, there will be worries that the extra attention given to literacy and numeracy in primary schools will marginalize health topics and reduce opportunities for children to gain knowledge and understanding about their bodies.

PE Lessons

Encouragement to increase the amount of physical activity in which young children are involved has come from policy documents such as *Labour's Sporting*

Nation (Labour Party 1996). The potential of physical education to promote school sport is recognized and the Labour Party has indicated that, central to their intention to reverse the decline of sport in schools, primary school teachers will continue to have a key role in ensuring that all children experience physical activities. However, despite this apparent commitment to physical activity, and additional support given by the Teacher Training Agency (1998), it is curious that in 1998 Key Stage 1 and 2 PE Programmes of Study were suspended until at least the year 2000 (Waring and Warburton, in press). Primary schools are still obliged to teach PE, but may decide what they teach and how often they teach it (DfEE 1998) and Ofsted are no longer required to report on PE curriculum content, being limited to commenting on PE lessons observed and extra-curricular opportunities provided by the school (Ofsted 1998).

This situation suggests that the government is mostly interested in performance-related school sport and is not genuinely committed to a broad and balanced PE curriculum or the promotion of active lifestyles among the wider primary school population. In contrast, support has come from the HEA in its statement that 'schools should develop the concept of the health-promoting school, which includes the contribution that physical activity can make to health' (1998: 8).

Telema, a renowned Finnish researcher, stated that:

> PE should enhance habitual physical activity and a healthy lifestyle and teach individuals how to take care of their fitness and health ... and should attend to the health development of students and support their mental well being and mental health while at school.
>
> (1997: 16)

Health-related exercise, which has become a prominent feature of school PE programmes, is 'a term used to encompass the understanding, skills and attitudes associated with the adoption of active lifestyles' (Harris and Cale 1997: 85). In many ways, health-related exercise is an unhelpful term since it focuses on the concept of 'exercise', which has a dubious role to play in the lifestyles of the general population. For many people, exercise is perceived negatively, giving rise to thoughts of unpleasant experiences undertaken for the instrumental purpose of getting fit.

The extent to which this topic has been included in primary school education is difficult to gauge. Harris and Cale (1997) undertook an extensive review of health-related physical education programmes, but close analysis shows that the few programmes conducted in UK primary schools consisted of very small samples of 10- and 11-year-olds receiving augmented PE programmes over a limited number of months. The main concern of these programmes seems to have been to promote short-term fitness gain rather than to encourage long-term active lifestyles.

Sallis and McKenzie (1991) considered that school physical education lessons provided the best opportunity to address the activity needs of virtually all children and this is a view supported by others reviewing the promotion of physical activity among young people (McGuinness et al. 1991; Morris 1991). However, it is necessary to examine the implications of this viewpoint. Does it mean that PE lessons should enable children to meet the HEA recommended physical activity threshold? This notion is clearly unrealistic because most children in UK primary schools do not experience PE lessons every day and, as mentioned earlier, there are a great many days of the year when children are not at school anyway.

Research in the USA (Simons-Morton et al. 1994; Faucette et al. 1990) has also indicated that children's physical activity levels during PE lessons were not as high as might be expected. This issue has also been examined in the UK by Sleap and Warburton (1996), who looked in considerable detail at PE lessons involving 5- to 11-year-olds. One hundred and seventy-eight PE lessons were monitored, consisting of 86 games lessons, 82 gymnastics and dance lessons and 10 swimming lessons. Ninety-two per cent of the children did not engage in at least one sustained 10-minute period of moderate intensity physical activity, while 69 per cent did not take part in at least one 5-minute bout of moderate intensity physical activity during the lessons. Additionally, it was found that an average of 23 per cent of PE lessons was spent passively listening, queuing, watching, sitting or standing. A follow-up study by Warburton and Woods (1996), involving 20 children and 36 PE lessons, established very similar physical activity patterns with 7- to 11-year-old children.

While many children have now been observed during primary school PE lessons, covering a wide range of activity areas, they are not representative of the tens of thousands of children experiencing PE lessons every week. Bearing this reservation in mind, the evidence to date appears to suggest that, as in the USA, children are not as physically active as might be expected. The question arises as to whether this should be a concern in terms of health promotion. An interesting point is made by Ofsted in a recent document:

> less confident teachers often find it easy to stimulate lots of movement activity in their classes, and believe that if pupils are active in physical education, they must be learning. Such uncontrolled movement is, however, as inappropriate in PE lessons as unstructured outpouring of words on to paper in English, or random brushstrokes in art.
>
> (Ofsted 1998: 4)

This observation illustrates the fallibility of promoting increased physical activity inappropriately. There is no evidence that shows any correlation between levels of physical activity in PE lessons and physical activity levels in adulthood. It is quite conceivable that children's future physical activity patterns might be positively influenced by relatively inactive PE lessons and vice versa. School drill

Figure 3.1 Ways of Maximizing Physical Activity Levels in PE Lessons

PLANNING	A well planned PE lesson can maximize physical activity opportunities for all children. For example, if transitions from one phase of a lesson to another are efficient, children can be quickly active and not waiting for groups to be re-organised or equipment to be re-positioned.
WARM UPS	Warm ups offer ideal opportunities for all children to be physically active. Fun and variety are the key elements – a jog around the playground every PE lesson is unlikely to inspire a love of physical activity. [See end of chapter for sources of ideas]
SPACE	Effective planning of available space will increase physical activity opportunities. For example, if group activities are appropriately spaced out, there will be fewer interruptions from children or equipment going astray from other groups.
EQUIPMENT	Small equipment like bats, balls and hoops are relatively inexpensive and, if in good supply, can save children waiting for long periods to get a turn. The best utilisation of small equipment also of course depends on careful planning of activities and effective use of space.
SMALL SIDED GAMES	One ball between 22 children = restricted physical activity. 2 v 2, 3 v 3, 4 v 4 and 5 v 5 all can lead to increased involvement, more fluent play, more skill development and a more rewarding physical activity experience for each child.

lessons in the early part of the century probably engaged young people in more physical activity than present-day PE lessons and yet the pain and discomfort of these lessons probably killed off any enthusiasm for or liking of physical activity for that generation. In other words, the quality of content of the PE lesson is likely to be the critical factor on this issue.

Harris and Cale summed up this point neatly: 'Rather than focusing on physical training, health-related physical education programmes should aim to impart the knowledge, understanding and skills necessary to lead a healthy, active lifestyle as well as foster positive attitudes towards physical activity' (1997: 97).

So, what might be included in PE lessons to encourage life-long participation in physical activity? Certainly, children need to understand why they should be active and how they can stay active, reinforcing health principles established in the classroom. Crucially, these early impressions of physical activity need to be positive – PE experiences need to be fun, exciting, challenging and rewarding. This is unlikely to be the case if children are embarrassed, bored, feel excessive pain or experience repeated failure.

If these positive principles are in place, it may also be appropriate to consider organising PE lessons to maximize physical activity levels for children. There will be benefits of this since, apart from other educational values (for example, increased skill development), children are more likely to enjoy their physical activity the more they are involved. A child who stands around waiting for a touch of the ball or a turn at the long jump may relate this negative experience to a dislike of physical activity in general. In addition, for children who engage in very little moderate intensity physical activity in other settings, the school PE lesson may be the one place where at least a small degree of physical activity is experienced (see Figure 3.1).

The Extended Curriculum

The extended curriculum offers further opportunities for the promotion of active lifestyles among children. While there is little comparative evidence from earlier times, it is a popular belief that extended curriculum activities declined during the 1980s and 1990s. Various sources have identified issues such as industrial action, increased workload and the withdrawal of voluntary support as reasons for reduced teacher involvement in the extended curriculum (Hill 1991; McStravick 1990; Labour Party 1996). While eminently valuable in many ways, extended curriculum activities in primary schools have mainly been limited to practices and matches for school sports teams, involving relatively small numbers of children. Thus, it is probable that this aspect of school life has never been significant in promoting physically active lifestyles among the majority of pupils.

One of the few pieces of evidence in the UK concerning extended curriculum activities in primary schools comes from a study by Warburton et al. (1991), which assessed participation in organized school club activities among 1,133 4- to 11-year-olds. Around half of the sample did not attend any kind of school club and most of the activities on offer were traditional sports which, while valuable in their own way, provide only a limited form of activity experience for young people.

A new approach

Primary schools could take an important stride forward in promoting active lifestyles by adopting an approach which appears at present to be quite rare. This would be to base the extended curriculum on a *recreational* approach to physical activities. In this context, activity opportunities would be open to all children, not just elite performers, and participation would be mainly focused on enjoyment and not competition.

While traditional sporting activities might still be available, consideration would be given to activities like chasing games, skipping activities, orienteering challenges, novelty relays, co-operative physical activities, circus skills, dancing to pop music and many others. The advantage of these types of activities is that all children can take part, minimal equipment is required and little specialist expertise is needed on the part of teachers or supervisors.

The TOPS programme

The TOPS programme is an initiative run by an organization called the Youth Sport Trust, which seeks to develop a 'sporting community' among young people. The initiative aims to develop and deliver quality sport programmes in schools and the community for young people aged 18 months to 18 years. It consists of many elements including in-service training for teachers, the setting up and running of out-of-school clubs and Sportsability, an inclusive games programme for young disabled people.

One of the key components of the TOPS programme is the development of a 'sporting community', both within and outside the school environment. National Lottery money will be invested through the New Opportunities Fund to increase the quality and quantity of out-of-school sports clubs. Schools will also be encouraged to share equipment and develop further sporting club activities by forming partnerships with other schools (for example, secondary schools with partner primary schools) and also by developing links in the community.

To date, high levels of satisfaction have been reported in relation to the equipment, resource cards and training for TOPS activities (Hunt 1998; Spode 1997), although the feedback is less positive in relation to links with other schools, clubs and agencies in the community. Research by Hooper (1998), Owen (1999) and Lewis (1999) indicates that teachers find links with other schools time-consuming and links with outside agencies problematic, in terms of the extra work involved. The philosophy of developing partnerships to extend the sporting curriculum is admirable in theory, but it would seem that it is far more difficult to operate in practice.

The TOPS programme is mainly focused on competitive sport and, consequently, will have a limited role in promoting active lifestyles among young people. Where the TOPS programme is inclusive and offers mass participation opportunities in sport, it will be most effective in encouraging young people to be physically active. Where there is a focus on elite performance, the aims will be different and there will be limited numbers of young people involved in physical activity.

Break and lunch time

Almost a quarter of a primary school child's day can be spent in break and lunch time and the potential for engaging in physical activity is therefore high. Bearing in mind earlier reservations about small sample sizes, the evidence indicates that, for many children, break and lunch time are more active than PE lessons or time at home.

Sleap and Warburton (1996) found that children took part in moderate intensity physical activity for approximately half of school break and lunch times. It will come as no surprise to many teachers that the most popular activities during these periods were football and chasing games. It should be emphasized that these times are averages and, while some children were very active, many others stood around or sat down for most, if not all, of these play-times.

Figure 3.2 illustrates the many different ways in which physical activity can be promoted at break and lunch times.

Concluding Comments

It has been maintained in this chapter that scaremongering about children's sedentary lifestyles is ill-conceived. The situation is quite confused and researchers have a lot to learn in terms of the relationship between young people, physical activity and health. Interventions to ameliorate disease risk factors through increased physical activity have proved inconclusive, and yet this does not mean that there should be complacency about children's activity behaviour.

First, there is a pressing need for a better picture of children's physical activity behaviour in the UK. This means that the full childhood age range must be studied and in sufficient numbers to warrant robust generalizations about the remainder of the childhood population. There needs to be continued efforts to understand the health implications of physically inactive lifestyles in youth and substantial endeavours to explore the tracking of childhood behaviour, through adolescence and into adulthood.

While some of the interpretations offered in this chapter differ from conventional wisdom about children's physical activity, it is the firm conviction of the authors that schools must, nevertheless, play a strong role in encouraging physically active lifestyles among their pupils. The tentacles of lethargy will continue into the new millennium and children must be given every opportunity to gain a healthy start which, in turn, can lead to a life of health-promoting and rewarding physical activity.

45

Figure 3.2   Maximizing Physical Activity at Break and Lunch Time

DESIGN OF SCHOOL GROUNDS	While many primary schools have extremely limited grounds, there are others which may offer greater physical activity opportunities than presently exist. For example, since playing fields can only be used at break and lunch times for a short period of the year, is there a case for extending the tarmac playground?
ZONING OF PLAYGROUND	Zoning involves the (temporary) allocation of playground areas to particular activities or groups of children. If appropriately planned, it can lead to a fair distribution of playground space and avoid the domination of areas by particular groups and certain physical activities.
PLAYGROUND MARKINGS	Colourful, creative playground markings are now available which can lead to inspired and imaginary active play. Children might be rabbits crossing a maze trying to avoid being caught by the wolf or they might be pirates attempting to steal the treasure from a deserted island drawn on a sea of waves.
TEACHING OF GAMES	Children nowadays may need help with ideas for active games. There are many resources available which adults can use – see end of chapter for sources. Another popular method is for older children to be given the opportunity of teaching younger children some of the games.
LUNCHTIME SUPERVISORS	Given suitable training and support, lunchtime supervisors can help children with active games. Their job can become more interesting since they can take on a positive, helpful role rather than being mainly concerned with discipline and punishment.
SMALL EQUIPMENT	While not suitable in all circumstances, the availability of small equipment at break and lunch times can add another dimension to children's physical activity. As long as strict management of the equipment is adopted, the fun, excitement and increased physical activity far outweigh the inevitable replacement costs.

Further Information

BRITISH HEART FOUNDATION

At The Heart of Education, Exercise and Heart Health
British Heart Foundation
14 Fitzhardinge Street
London W1H 4DH
UK

THE HAPPY HEART PROJECT

Research Unit for PE, Sport and Health
Institute for Learning
University of Hull
Hull HU6 7RX
UK

JUMP ROPE FOR HEART

Jump Rope for Heart Coordinator
Department of PE, Sports Science and Recreational Management
Loughborough University
Loughborough LE11 3TU
UK

'ACTION FOR HEART HEALTH' (J. HARRIS AND J. ELBOURN, 1991)

Loughborough University
Loughborough LE11 3TU
UK

THE TOPS PROGRAMME

The Youth Sport Trust
Rutland Building
Loughborough University
Loughborough, LE11 3TU
UK

References

Armstrong, N. (1998) 'Physical education, sport and the promotion of children's health and well-being' in A.J. Sargeant and H. Siddons (eds) *From Community Health to Elite*

47

Sport. Proceedings of Third Annual Congress of the European College of Sport Science, 15–18 July. Liverpool: Centre for Health Care Development.

Armstrong, N. and Welsman, J. (1997) *Young People and Physical Activity.* Oxford: Oxford University Press.

Bailey, R.C., Olson, J., Pepper, S.L., Porszasz, J., Barstow, T.J. and Cooper, D.M. (1995) 'The level and tempo of children's physical activities: an observational study', *Medicine and Science in Sports and Exercise* 27, 1033–41.

Baranowski, T. (1988) 'Validity and reliability of self-report of physical activity: an information-processing perspective', *Research Quarterly* 59, 314–27.

Baranowski, T., Hooks, P., Tsong, Y., Cieslik, C. and Nader: R. (1987) 'Aerobic physical activity among third- to sixth-grade children', *Journal of Developmental Behavioral Pediatrics* 8, 203–6.

Blair, S.N. (1993) '1993 C.H. McCloy Research Lecture: Physical activity, physical fitness and health', *Research Quarterly* 64, 365–76.

Bouchard, C., Shephard, R. and Stephens, T., (1994) (eds) *Physical Activity, Fitness, and Health: International proceedings and consensus statement.* Champaign, IL: Human Kinetics.

Cale, L. (1998) 'Monitoring young people's physical activity', *British Journal of Physical Education* 29, 28–31.

DfE (1990) *Curriculum Guidance 5: Health education.* York: National Curriculum Council.

——(1995) *Key Stages 1 and 2 of the National Curriculum.* London: HMSO.

DfEE (1998) 'Blunkett strengthens curriculum focus on the basics', *DES News 006/98* 13 January. London: HMSO.

DeBusk, R.F., Stenestrand, U., Sheehan, M. and Haskell, W.L. (1990) 'Training effects of long versus short bouts of exercise in healthy subjects', *American Journal of Cardiology* 65, 1010–13.

Faucette, N., Mckenzie, T.L. and Patterson, N. (1990) 'Descriptive analysis of non-specialist elementary teachers' curricula choices in class organisation', *Journal of Teaching in Physical Education* 9, 284–93.

Glenmark, B., Healberg, G. and Jansson, E. (1994) 'Prediction of physical activity level in adulthood by physical characteristics, physical performance and physical activity in adolescence: an 11-year follow-up study', *European Journal of Applied Physiology* 69, 530–8.

Harris, J. and Cale, L. (1997) 'How healthy is school PE? A review of the effectiveness of health-related physical education programmes in schools', *Health Education Journal* 56, 84–104.

Haskell, W.L. (1994) 'Health consequences of physical activity', *Medicine and Science in Sports and Exercise*, 26, 649–60.

Health Education Authority (HEA) (1997) *Young People and Physical Activity: A literature review.* London: Health Education Authority.

——(1998)*Young and Active: Policy framework for young people and health-enhancing physical activity.* London: Health Education Authority.

Hill, J. (1991) 'Sport and extra-curricular activity – some issues', *British Journal of Physical Education* 22, 33–4.

Hooper, M. (1998) 'Monitoring TOP Play and BT Top Sport with Dudley LEA', *Bulletin of Physical Education*, 34, 49–54.

Hunt, M. (1998) 'Top Play and BT Top Sport: An effective influence on teaching?', *Bulletin of Physical Education* 34, 194–205.

Kuh, D.J.L. and Cooper, C. (1992) 'Physical activity at 36 years: patterns and childhood predictors in a longitudinal study', *Journal of Epidemiology and Community Health* 46, 114–19.

Labour Party (1996) *Labour's Sporting Nation*. London: the Labour Party.

Lewis, D. (1999) 'An assessment of the effectiveness of Top Play and BT Top Sport in County Durham with suggestions for the enhancement and development of the programme'. Unpublished dissertation, University of Durham.

McGuinness, J.M., Kanner, L. and Degraw, C. (1991) 'Physical education's role in achieving national health objectives', *Research Quarterly for Exercise and Sport* 62, 138–42.

McStravick, B. (1990) 'Athletics: from the school to the club', *British Journal of Physical Education* 21, 279–80.

Morris, H.H. (1991) 'The role of school physical education in public health, *Research Quarterly for Exercise and Health* 62, 143–7.

Morris, J.N., Everitt, M.G., Pollard, R. and Chave, S.P.W. (1980) 'Vigorous exercise in leisure-time: protection against coronary heart disease', *The Lancet* 2, 1207–10.

Ofsted (1998) *Inspecting Subjects 3–11: Guidance for inspections*. London: Ofsted.

Owen, R.C. (1999) 'The effectiveness of Top Play and BT Top Sport in the primary schools of County Durham'. Unpublished dissertation, University of Durham.

Paffenbarger, R.S., Wing, A.L. and Hyde, R.T. (1978) 'Physical activity as an index of heart attack risk in college alumni', *American Journal of Epidemiology* 108, 161–75.

Riddoch, C. (1998) 'Relationships between physical activity and physical health in young people', in S. Biddle, J. Sallis and N. Cavill (eds) *Young and Active?* London: Health Education Authority, 17–48.

Sallis, J.F. and McKenzie, T.L. (1991) 'Physical education's role in public health', *Research Quarterly* 62, 124–37.

Shropshire J., and Carroll, R. (1998) 'Final year primary school children's physical activity levels and choices, *European Journal of Physical Education* 3, 156–66.

Simons-Morton, B.G., Taylor, W.C., Snider, S.A., Huang, I.W. and Fulton, J.E. (1994) 'Observed level of elementary and middle school children's physical activity during physical education classes', *Preventive Medicine* 23, 437–41.

Sleap, M. (1997) 'Promoting active lifestyles among children', *Social Sciences in Health* 3, 232–43.

Sleap, M. and Warburton, P. (1996) 'Physical activity levels of 5–11-year-old children in England: cumulative evidence from three direct observation studies', *International Journal of Sports Medicine* 17, 248–53.

Spode, I. (1997) 'An evaluative case study into the effect Top Play and Top Sport has had on the quality of teaching and pupil responses within eight primary schools', *Bulletin of Physical Education* 33, 42–9.

Teacher Training Agency (1998) *National Standards for Subject Leaders*. London: Teacher Training Agency.

Telema, R. (1997) 'Physical education and the health of the nation – a Finnish perspective', in School Curriculum and Assessment Authority, *Physical Education and the Health of the Nation*. London: SCAA.

Telema, R., Viikari, J., Valimaki, I., Siren-Tiusanen, H., Akerblom, H.K., Uhari, M., Dahl, M., Pesonen, E., Lahde, P.L. Pietkainen, M., and Suoinen, P. (1985)

'Atherosclerosis precursors in Finnish children and adolescents. X. Leisure time physical activity, *Acta Paediatrica Scandinavica (supplement)* 318, 169–80.

Thirlaway, K. and Benton, D. (1993) 'Physical activity in primary and secondary school children in West Glamorgan', *Health Education Journal* 52, 37–41.

Warburton, P., Sleap, M. and Williams, R. (1991) 'Participation in organised physical activities by children aged 4–11 years', *British Journal of PE Research Supplement* 10, 2–4.

Warburton, P. and Woods, J. (1996) 'Observation of children's activity levels during primary school physical education lessons', *European Journal of Physical Education* 1, 56–65.

Waring, M. and Warburton, P. (in press) 'Working with the community: a necessary evil or a positive change of direction?', in S. Capel and S. Piotrowski (eds) *Issues in Physical Education*. London: Routledge.

4　Physical Education and Health-Promoting Primary Schools

Sue Piotrowski

Introduction

This chapter focuses on the findings of three small-scale case studies that were conducted in Health-Promoting School Award (HPSA) winning primary schools in East Kent. The purpose of the case studies was to investigate the extent to which Physical Education (PE) and a focus on physical activity featured in the health-promoting ethos and practices of these award-winning schools. This case-study evidence draws attention to several examples of good practice with respect to the promotion of health-enhancing physical activity in the schools visited. However, the evidence also suggests that, to date, the specific focus on PE and the involvement of specialist trained PE professionals in the HPSA schemes in primary schools has been limited. The implications of these findings for policy and practice in primary school PE will be considered with reference to the recommended levels of physical activity for young people (5–18 years) recently published by the Health Education Authority (HEA) (1998).

Background to Health-Promoting School Award Schemes

The Health-Promoting School initiative is based on a settings-based approach to health promotion, of the kind first encouraged by the World Health Organization's *Ottawa Charter* (WHO 1986). Health was considered too important to be left solely to medical practitioners and it was emphasized that education and policy development would need to play a central role in individual, community and national health. It is an approach which underpins the public health movements that have developed internationally, for example 'Healthy Cities' and 'Health Promotion in the Workplace'.

A settings-based approach to health promotion differs from a medical model of health promotion, where emphasis is placed on the individual and which might be described, to use Holland's words, as 'an essentially victim blaming approach' (1995: 12). Instead, a settings-based approach acknowledges both (i) the importance of the environmental context as a major influence on health and (ii) causal factors pertaining to the individual and his/her behaviour. In other words, the settings approach recognizes both the structural (fiscal/ecological) element and the individual (behavioural) element as two key aspects to improving health.

The health-promoting school is based on a holistic concept of health, where concern is with 'the total individual in the total environment' (Jensen 1992). A health-promoting school seeks to promote the health of the school community within the whole school environment. The school community includes not just pupils but also teachers and support staff and the groups, including families and others, with whom they interact in the wider community. Within the school, 'all aspects of school life in addition to the taught curriculum should demonstrate that health is considered to be of utmost importance to everyone' (Holland 1995: 2).

The Council of Europe (CE), Commission of the European Communities (CEC) and the WHO (1995) defined the Health Promoting School as follows:

> The Health Promoting School aims at achieving healthy lifestyles for the total school population by developing supportive environments conducive to the promotion of health. It offers opportunities for, and requires commitments to, the provision of a safe and health-enhancing environment.
> (World Health Organization, Regional Office for Europe 1995)

In 1985 the CE, CEC and the WHO worked together to conduct pilot projects in schools based on this holistic view of health. These project schools were acknowledged at the 'European Conference on the Promotion of Health Education' to have demonstrated the importance of the school as a setting for health education programmes. The European Network for Health Promoting Schools was established, with the first countries accepted in 1992. The United Kingdom was accepted into the Network in September 1993 and the project in England is managed by the HEA.

Alongside the national project, a variety of independent HPSA schemes has been developed by Health Promotion Units across the country. These projects include an East Kent HPSA scheme which was established in 1995. The working group for the scheme included representatives from the local Health Promotion Unit, Kent County Constabulary, a secondary school, the Road Safety Department, The Kent Curriculum Services Agency, Environmental Health, and an area manager of School Nurses. The working group invited applications from local schools interested in gaining a health-promoting school award. To qualify for the award, and with it the privilege of using the health-promoting school logo on school stationery, schools were required to demonstrate their progress towards meeting the aims of the HPSA initiative through meeting a number of criteria.

The aim of the HPSA scheme was to encourage 'schools to make school life a health-promoting experience for all pupils and staff who teach, learn and work in it' (HPS Working Group 1996: 3). In working towards this end, schools were required to meet the following ten criteria.

Health-Promoting School Award scheme

Criteria – A health-promoting school should:

1 Enable and encourage pupils to make decisions about, take charge of and value their own health.
2 Have a health and sex education policy. It should have a structured and developmental programme. 'Curriculum Guidance 5' should form the basis of the programme which should be co-ordinated and reflected in the School Development Plan.
3 Demonstrate a commitment to encourage positive attitudes to health in the wider community and give opportunities for consultation and involvement of parents, governors, health authorities and other interested groups. This should be a two way relationship with involvement of the school in wider community activities.
4 Promote the self-esteem of all members of the school community.
5 Ensure that there is equal opportunity and access to health education for all who teach, learn and work in the school.
6 Be working towards a smoke free environment.
7 Show evidence of promoting a clean, safe and stimulating environment which includes having a Road Safety Policy. The school should operate with due consideration to the pupils, staff and visitors.
8 Encourage a positive attitude towards health related activities and offer a range of physical and recreational activities for all.
9 Provide healthy choices in eating areas, and these areas should promote healthy eating.
10 Provide toilets which are kept clean with washing facilities, adequate stocks of paper, hand dryers and hand towels. Cubicles must be secure.

(HPS Working Group 1996: 4)

To assist the schools in meeting the criteria, a list of performance indicators were specified in relation to each criterion. In relation to Criterion 8, which places emphasis on health-related physical activity, the performance indicators were identified as follows.

Criterion 8: A positive attitude to health related activities should be encouraged by providing a range of physical and recreational activities for all

Performance indicators

Does the school:

8a Make links between Health Education and PE?
8b Ensure that curricular and a range of extra curricular opportunities are available for all pupils?
8c Encourage pupils and staff to make informed decisions about a wide range of physical and recreational activities?
8d Use local recreational facilities where possible if facilities are not available on site?
8e Make pupils and staff aware of the benefits of exercise as a means of reducing stress?
8f Acknowledge out-of-school success in physical recreational activities?
8g Provide adequate opportunities for staff to relax during non-contact time?

(HPS Working Group 1996: 12)

The case-study data included in this chapter is based on findings from three primary schools that were successful in gaining a HPSA from the East Kent scheme. The purpose of the case studies was to focus on the extent to which an emphasis on physical activity, and in particular the extent to which PE within and beyond the school curriculum, was integrated into the ethos and practices of the HPSA scheme. Criterion 8 ensures that the physical activity dimension of the health of the school community is not ignored by schools seeking the HPSA. But how is this focus on physical activity manifested in practice? What is the reality behind the rhetoric?

Small-Scale Case Studies of Three HPSA Winning Primary Schools: The Physical Activity Dimension

Research Methodology

Three primary schools in the East Kent region were selected for study because of their recent success in gaining the HPSA. The author made a half-day visit to each of the selected schools during June and July 1997. The research methodology employed was mainly qualitative. A multi-focused methodology was used for data collection including: analysis of documentary evidence relating to PE and the implementation of the HPSA scheme within the school; semi-structured interviews with the health education co-ordinator in each school; and observation of practices, including pupil and staff behaviour within the school.

The interview schedule with the health education co-ordinators used a series of questions focused on three main themes:

(i)   The impact of involvement in the HPSA scheme on curricular PE;

(ii)   The impact of involvement in the HPSA scheme on extra-curricular PE, physical activity and recreation;

(iii) The integration of PE/physical activity in general health-promoting events, for example school health week.

The interviews were conducted in a relaxed, conversational manner. To retain the relaxed, open and frank manner in which the health co-ordinators were willing to converse, the interviews were not tape-recorded but brief notes were kept by the interviewer of the content of the discussions. Immediately following the visits, a detailed version of the notes made during the visit was produced. These detailed records provided the data for analysis. The analysis of the data was guided by the aim of the research. This was to ascertain the extent to which the formal PE curriculum, or a more general focus on physical activity within the school, explicitly contributed to the ethos and practices of the health-promoting school.

Case-Study Findings

Case study 1

THE SCHOOL

School One is a County Primary School with 272 pupils aged 5–11 years. The school comprises a two-storey building built in the early 1900s. The ward in which the school is located is one of the poorest in the country and has the highest proportion of children on the Social Services 'at risk' register in Kent. Eighty per cent of the pupils at the school have emotional, behavioural or learning difficulties. A considerable proportion of the children are from low-income families – reflected in the fact that 50 per cent of the pupils are eligible for free school meals. Health education is taught as part of the science curriculum supported by the whole school environment, which is used to promote health in the pupils' everyday experience.

This school was one of six schools included in Holland's (1995) more general evaluation of a local HPSA scheme. Holland's study included distribution of a questionnaire to the teaching staff and health education co-ordinator at School

One. Teachers were asked to estimate the school's level of achievement in relation to the scheme criteria. In relation to the performance indicators for Criterion 8, the teachers were asked to estimate the school's level of achievement using a five-point scale (where 5 = good; 1 = poor). The teaching staff displayed a generally high level of confidence with regard to the role of the school in encouraging a positive attitude to health-related activities and providing a range of physical and recreational activities for all. However, their scores in relation to performance indicators 8b – the range of curricular and extra-curricular activities and 8d – the use of outside recreational facilities, were below the average scores of teachers from the other five schools included in Holland's evaluation.

However, when the teaching staff of School One were asked by Holland to rank the ten criteria according to what they believed to be of most importance, they ranked concerns for physical activity as seventh in importance after an emphasis on hygienic toilets, general cleanliness and safety, healthy eating, raising pupil self-esteem, sex education, and developing pupil decision-making skills. Other schools included in the evaluation had ranked an emphasis on physical activity as second in importance (a secondary school); third in importance (a primary school); fourth in importance (a primary school); eighth in importance (a secondary school); and tenth in importance (a secondary school). Criterion 8, with its emphasis on physical activity, was not included amongst those which four or more schools believed to be of 'very great importance'.

In questionnaires administered by Holland (1995) to twenty-seven pupils at School One, sporting activities and healthy food were the two most frequently mentioned aspects that were considered to contribute to a healthy school. However, the absence of pollution was cited by the pupils as being the most important aspect of health. Eighty-one per cent of the pupils were able to contribute ideas on how to make their school healthier. None of the suggestions related to raising physical activity levels. Holland found a clear correlation between pupils' awareness of the importance of a healthy environment and the extent of their involvement in action to improve the health-promoting practices of the school. Pupils gave examples of their involvement in developing a healthy tuck shop, initiating a sponsored litter pick, and writing to a company to get 'a frog bin to make infants more keen to put their rubbish in the bin' (Holland 1995: 85).

When the seven support staff at the school and a sample of nine parents were asked by Holland (1995) to identify areas where the school was performing less well in relation to the criteria, no mention was made by parents of concerns relating to Criterion 8 and the promotion of physical activity. Instead, the parents' greatest concern was about the quality of school meals. However, the support staff within the school did consider the range of curricular and extra-curricular activities available at the school for physical and recreational activities to be a matter of particular concern.

In general, Holland (1995) found great value to be attached by pupils, staff and parents to the HPSA scheme. This was largely attributed to the personal involvement and degree of enthusiasm for the scheme from the headteacher and health education co-ordinator. The headteacher at School One considered the health education co-ordinator to be the 'key thing' to the success of the scheme. The headteacher is quoted by Holland: 'She [the health education co-ordinator] keeps the children enthusiastic who enthuse to other members of staff which keeps the whole thing going along' (1995: 83).

Compared to the other five schools included in Holland's (1995) evaluation, School One was found to be furthest ahead in its implementation of the scheme.

THE CONTRIBUTION OF THE PE CURRICULUM TO THE AIMS OF THE HEALTH-PROMOTING SCHOOL

From the author's own case-study investigations it was found that the school does not have a member of staff with specialist training in PE to co-ordinate policy and provision for this subject. The school does not have a policy document for PE. Nevertheless, the co-ordinator for health education recognizes the valuable contribution to be made by PE to children's health. Key Stage One (KS1) pupils (aged 5–7 years) have a daily half-hour session of PE, whilst Key Stage Two (KS2) children (aged 7–11 years) have three sessions per week with an extra session in the summer for swimming in the school's own outdoor pool. When asked what was being done to ensure that the PE curriculum was making an appropriate contribution to the health-promoting aims of the school, the response from the health education co-ordinator was, 'It is difficult to know. Without a PE policy document, each teacher in the school is doing their own thing'.

However, it was felt that all the teachers would be keen to promote the view that the efforts of all pupils are valued in PE curriculum sessions and children of all abilities are chosen to demonstrate their performance.

THE CONTRIBUTION OF EXTRA-CURRICULAR PHYSICAL ACTIVITY TO THE AIMS OF THE HPS

The health education co-ordinator describes the children as 'very unfit'. In an effort to address this, she encouraged the children to take part in a British Heart Foundation sponsored skip. A student play-leader is employed by the school at £5 an hour to organize lunch-time extra-curricular sports clubs for netball, cricket, dance, football and 'keep fit'. The school has managed to raise £100 in sponsorship from a local pharmaceuticals company to buy equipment such as skipping ropes, netball rings, and balls which can be used by pupils in free play during breaks.

THE FOCUS ON PE/PHYSICAL ACTIVITY DURING SPECIAL HPS EVENTS

During a special 'Health Week' at school, children were encouraged to try new sports such as trampolining and orienteering.

Case study 2

THE SCHOOL

School Two is a County Primary School for 318 pupils aged 5–11 years. The school was built in 1995. It has excellent facilities, which include a large playing field and two school halls. The school recently received an excellent report from Ofsted inspectors and has been proposed as a 'model school'. Less than 20 per cent of pupils have special educational needs.

THE CONTRIBUTION OF THE PE CURRICULUM TO THE AIMS OF THE HEALTH-PROMOTING SCHOOL

At the time of visiting the school (prior to the Ofsted visit!) the PE policy was not written, even though the school had achieved the HPSA. KS1 and KS2 classes had three time-tabled periods of PE a week – each of 40 minutes. The health education co-ordinator would like to see this increased to 40 minutes per day. One of the difficulties affecting increased PE provision is that only one of the school halls is available for all ten classes at the school. This one hall is also used for school lunches and school assemblies. The other hall is permanently used as a computer room.

THE CONTRIBUTION OF EXTRA-CURRICULAR PHYSICAL ACTIVITY TO THE AIMS OF THE HPS

Several extra-curricular PE clubs took place after school. A staggered lunch break made it difficult for any lunch-time clubs to take place.

The playground had been marked for a 'trim trail', which involved a circuit of exercises including squat thrusts, etc. that pupils could choose to follow. An after-school aerobics club was attended by both staff and pupils for 1 hour each week. The staff included support staff – the caretaker and a classroom assistant.

As with School One, this school had successfully secured £100 sponsorship from the same pharmaceuticals company to purchase balls, skittles and skipping ropes to encourage break-time physical activity.

THE FOCUS ON PE/PHYSICAL ACTIVITY DURING SPECIAL HPS EVENTS

During the school's 'Healthy Living Week', pupils took part in a sponsored jog around the school field.

Case study 3

THE SCHOOL

School Three is a County Infant School for 270 infant pupils aged 5–7 years. The school was built towards the end of the nineteenth century. Approximately 40 per cent of the pupils have special educational needs. The school has one hall, which is used for lunch and for school assemblies.

THE CONTRIBUTION OF THE PE CURRICULUM TO THE AIMS OF THE HEALTH-
PROMOTING SCHOOL

The school has a PE policy but it was not written by a teacher with specialist training in PE. The teacher responsible for drafting the policy document was the health education co-ordinator, who has a degree in French and a co-ordinating responsibility in the school for English. Every class has three sessions of curriculum PE per week. These include a 30-minute lesson for large apparatus work and two 20-minute sessions for dance and games.

THE CONTRIBUTION OF EXTRA-CURRICULAR PHYSICAL ACTIVITY TO THE AIMS OF
THE HPS

An after-school fitness club has been introduced for Year 2 pupils on Tuesdays and Thursdays. Approximately forty children from a year group of ninety children regularly attend the club, where they engage in 'rigorous exercise' for approximately 30 minutes. Teachers are pleased that the club has managed to attract some of the 'tubby children'. They have also commented on the perceived improvement in children's levels of fitness (stamina and flexibility) within PE curriculum sessions for those children who regularly attend the fitness club. Some parents have complained that the KS2 schools to which many of these children progress have no similar clubs for the children to continue their involvement.

THE FOCUS ON PE/PHYSICAL ACTIVITY WITHIN THE WIDER CONTEXT OF THE
SCHOOL

As part of the holistic emphasis on the health of the school community, the local health promotion unit tested the fitness of all school teaching and support staff. Following this, several staff now regularly swim together at the local pool.

Case-Study Conclusions

A common feature of the schools visited was that despite all three schools being HPSA winners, not one of these schools had a PE co-ordinator. Only one of the schools had a PE policy document and even in this one case it had been written by a teacher who has had no specialist training in teaching PE.

All three health education co-ordinators perceived lack of space as a difficulty in ensuring that the pupils had sufficient curriculum PE time in which to benefit their health. Even in the new school, which had two halls to accommodate pupil numbers, the additional space had been prioritized for computer use.

The content of the National Curriculum was also identified as posing a problem for promoting sufficient levels of physical activity in PE lessons. This was suggested to be due to the required emphasis on 'learning skills' to participate in various activity areas identified for inclusion at KS1 and KS2: namely, dance, games and gymnastics (plus athletics, outdoor and adventurous activities and swimming at KS2).

Commendable as many of the practices are to promote increased levels of physical activity, it is a matter of some concern that there is no involvement from anyone with specialist training in PE, either within the three schools or on the local HPSA Working Group, to advise on suitable levels of activity for young children. School Three is proud of its efforts in involving 6-year-old pupils in rigorous non-stop strenuous exercise for 20 to 25 minutes. This 'achievement' is reported in the local Health-Promoting newsletter (Donelan 1996), which is designed to share good practice with other participating schools in the local health promoting school scheme. But where are those with appropriate expertise in the paediatric exercise sciences to offer guidance on the suitability of this level of intensity for pupils of this age? Harris and Cale's (1997: 61) cautionary note that it is possible for acknowledgement of children's low activity levels to result in unsuitable forms of 'vigorous exercise being promoted at the expense of less strenuous forms of exercise' may be a salutary reminder in this and similar contexts.

Implications for Primary School PE

HEA Recommendations for Health-Enhancing Physical Activity for Children

The implications of these case-study findings for primary PE can be considered in the context of recent recommendations from the HEA (1998) concerning the amount and type of physical activity in which young people, including children aged 5–11 years, should engage if health benefits are to follow. The HEA (1998: 1) acknowledge that whilst in relation to the adult population there is 'strong international consensus that building up to half an hour a day of moderate intensity activity, like brisk walking, is beneficial for health', the evidence base for children is much weaker. A strong consensus from the scientific community has yet to emerge on the minimal and optimal amount of physical activity for children and young people aged 5–18 years. Nevertheless, a review of the evidence by the HEA which began in June 1997, coupled with a process of expert consultation, strongly supports the HEA's primary and secondary recommendations concerning the amount and intensity of physical activity for a health-enhancing effect for children to follow. These recommendations are as follows:

HEA (1998) Recommendations for promoting health-enhancing physical activity with young people (5–18 years):

Primary recommendation:

- All young people should participate in physical activity of at least moderate intensity for *one hour a day.*
- Young people who currently do little activity should participate in physical activity of at least moderate intensity for *at least half an hour per day.*

Secondary recommendation:

At least twice a week, some of these activities should help to enhance and maintain muscular strength and flexibility, and bone health.

Examples of moderate intensity physical activities, suggested by the HEA, include: brisk walking; cycling; swimming; most sports and dance. The activity can be continuous or intermittently accumulated throughout the day. The contexts in which the activity can occur are varied and can include: transportation (e.g. walking or cycling to and from school); curricular and extra-curricular PE; physical recreation; work; structured exercise or active play. It is not necessary to engage in high-intensity, rigorous exercise for health benefits to follow.

The HEA (1998) identify current and future beneficial health outcomes for children who engage in the recommended levels of physical activity. These outcomes include benefits for current levels of physical fitness, health and well-being, growth and development; the development of active lifestyles that can be maintained throughout life; and the reduced risk of chronic diseases of adulthood.

Combining Physical Activity with other Health-Enhancing Behaviour

The realization of the health benefits identified above is often dependent on appropriate levels of physical activity being maintained in combination with other health-enhancing behaviours. For example, regular engagement in the

61

recommended levels of physical activity can reduce obesity – when combined with appropriate dietary modification. Physical activity can have a beneficial effect on self-esteem providing the psychological benefits are not limited by an over-emphasis on competitive performance. Similarly, the risk of coronary heart disease (CHD), which is one of the chronic diseases of adulthood, is higher where there is a lack of exercise but there are other risk factors such as smoking and poor blood-fat profiles (Bird 1992). For physical activity to have a health-enhancing effect, it is best considered in combination with other health-promoting behaviours.

Not surprisingly, the HEA encourages the education sector, including primary schools, to adopt a whole-school approach to promoting physical activity. HPSA schemes, of the kind described in this chapter, provide an ideal vehicle through which to ensure that adequate attention is given to the physical activity needs of the pupils in conjunction with their other health needs.

Primary PE and the Health-Promoting School

The National Curriculum for PE (DfE 1995), through the general programmes of study, requires that the subject is used to 'promote physical activity and healthy lifestyles'. More recently, the proposals for a revised National Curriculum (QCA 1999: 5) acknowledge the general role of the school curriculum, and more specifically the PE curriculum, in encouraging pupils 'to recognise the importance of pursuing a healthy lifesyle.' In relation to proposals for a revised National Curriculum for PE, part of the distinctive contribution of PE is suggested to lie in enabling pupils 'to discover and come to terms with their own aptitudes, preferences and make decisions about how to get involved in active and healthy lifestyles' (QCA 1999: 170). This is more likely to be achieved where PE is integrated into a whole-school approach to the health of the school community so that a range of potentially health-enhancing and health-threatening behaviours are given appropriate consideration.

If primary teachers are to be effective in encouraging pupils to engage in recommended levels of physical activity, it is important that they develop an awareness of some of the determinants affecting the involvement of children in physical activity. The HEA (1998) suggest these determinants to include: the perceived enjoyment of the activities; consistent association between some key psychological variables (such as feelings of competence) and physical activity; the impact of the media, gender and socio-cultural variables on participation in physical activity. An implication for structured programmes of PE in health-promoting primary schools is to look to promote those elements which have been linked to a motivation to participate in physical activity (such as maximizing the enjoyment of participation in physical activity for all pupils and enhancing feelings of physical competence and mastery for all). On the other hand, physical educators should look for ways to overcome obstacles, such as socio-economic barriers, to participation. This may require challenging those gender stereotypes that may inhibit greater involvement, particularly by girls in many team sports and by boys in some of the more aesthetic pursuits such as dance and gymnastics.

In promoting healthy lifestyles, encouraging pupils to engage in recommended levels of physical activity is important. However, health-related goals in PE are not only about encouraging pupils to be currently active but also about seeking to develop attitudes toward physical activity that will promote life-long participation. In this respect the ethos of the health-promoting school may be significant to achieving this goal. The approach of the health-promoting school, with its emphasis on self-empowerment and the involvement of pupils in making decisions that affect their own health status, may have a positive effect in developing active lifestyles in children that are maintained into adulthood. Baric (1992) cites research which suggests that using a settings approach to health promotion that enables people to increase control and improve their own health is likely to have a lasting effect. Abdelgadir's study of Sudanese villages found that empowering community members with the responsibility for their own well-being and equipping them with the competencies for dealing with problems within their own limits had a positive influence on the lasting effect of community changes. Similarly, Holland's (1995) evaluation of a local health-promoting school award scheme found a correlation between the involvement of pupils in action to improve their school and the degree of importance attached by those pupils to a healthy environment. It would be an interesting area for further research, for example through longitudinal studies, to see whether these more positive attitudes towards the need for a healthy environment are retained into adulthood.

The goal of encouraging pupils to pursue healthy lifestyles is also more likely to be achieved when schools and the community provide mutually supporting contexts for health-enhancing behaviours. The health-promoting school can provide opportunities for those with a specialist interest in promoting appropriate levels of physical activity to work with other key personnel from the school and local community in fostering opportunities for regular involvement in physical activity of moderate intensity throughout the day. For example, if pupils are to be encouraged to walk or cycle to school there will need to be liaison with community officials to ensure the provision of safe routes. Within the school, there will need to be secure storage facilities both for cycles and cycle helmets.

Involving parents and guardians in an attempt to establish continuity between health-promoting behaviours encouraged within the school with those at home is another important link between the health-promoting school and the community. These links are particularly significant in the case of health-enhancing physical activity, since there is substantial evidence (HEA 1998) that there is a correlation between family and peer support and the physical activity levels of young people. In an evaluation of the European Network of Health-Promoting Schools, Parsons et al. (1997) found evidence from schools visited in Lithuania, Ireland and Romania of successful attempts to involve parents in physical activity within the school. In one Lithuanian school, the headteacher exercised with parents and teachers. The parents also used the school facilities at weekends to participate in sports competitions. One Irish school was found to have subsidized a parent and pupil swimming course. In Romania, the parents had built a mini-handball pitch at one school to increase the children's levels of physical activity.

In order for primary PE to be integrated into a more holistic approach to pupils' health, greater emphasis will need to be given to the potential contribution of primary PE in teacher training and continuing professional development courses. Action needs to be taken where there are schools, like those included in the case studies identified in this chapter, which do not have personnel within the school with specialist training in PE (to the level of a subject leader). PE and sport science departments of higher education institutions (HEIs) and other in-service providers, including LEA advisers, might offer specialist training in meeting the physical activity needs of children for primary school health education co-ordinators. This may focus attention more sharply on a variety of ways in which schools can look to apply the primary and secondary HEA (1998) recommendations for health-enhancing physical activity to all primary-aged children. It can also help to avoid the introduction of inappropriate over-rigorous regimes and help, through the development of greater expertise, to minimize one of the acknowledged negative effects of physical activity – that of increased risk of musculo-skeletal injury.

Conclusion

An implication of the case-study research detailed in this chapter is that primary school PE teachers, particularly those with subject-leader responsibilities, should be looking to play a more active part in health-promoting school initiatives. They should be assisted in their task through appropriate initial teacher training and continuing professional development opportunities that enable them to develop the necessary expertise to make a worthwhile contribution.

The school PE policy should be evident in all schools achieving 'health promoting school' status. It should detail the part to be played by curricular and extra-curricular PE in reaching HEA (1998) primary and secondary recommendations. This will include attention to the role to be played by structured programmes of PE in making a general contribution to the target of 1 hour a day of physical activity of at least moderate intensity. It should also document how opportunities are to be provided, at least twice a week where possible, for participation in activities which enhance and maintain muscular strength and flexibility. Schools achieving health promoting school status should also be expected to show how the formal curriculum is supported by extra-curricular opportunities for participation in physical activity. Both the delivery of curricular and extra-curricular provision should be prompted by an aim to facilitate lifelong participation in physical activity. The inclusion of pupils in decision-making processes about how they can best achieve an hour a day of physical activity is desirable since research (for example by Abdelgadir, cited in Baric 1992; Holland 1995) suggests that the message is likely to be received with greater significance and commitment.

By working within the context of a health-promoting school, the PE curriculum has a more realistic chance of meeting the National Curriculum requirement to promote healthy lifestyles. The ethos and practices of the school should ensure that other health-risk behaviour such as those associated with poor diet or smoking, for example, are also addressed. This allows any increases in the levels of health-enhancing physical activity to have maximum impact on the health of the school community. Liaison between the school and the outside community, including liaison with parents, can also help to ensure that the messages communicated by the school are consistent and reinforced by those of the family.

A conscious effort should be made by the teachers of PE in primary schools and health education co-ordinators to work together both within the school and with other agencies in the community to find the most appropriate ways of assisting all pupils to engage in appropriate levels of health-enhancing physical activity. The case study evidence presented in this chapter suggests that whilst there is much commendable health-enhancing activity taking place in primary schools under the umbrella of the HPSA scheme, there is considerable scope for greater involvement from those with specialist training and interests in PE.

References

Baric, L. (1992) 'Promoting health: new approaches and developments', *Journal of the Institute for Health Education* 30, 1, 6–16.

Bird, S. (1992) *Exercise Physiology for Health Professionals*. London: Chapman & Hall.

DfE (1995) *Physical Education in the National Curriculum*. London: HMSO.

Donelan, C. (ed.) (1996) *The Health Promoting School Newsletter* issue no. 3, July.

Harris, J. and Cale, L. (1997) Activity promotion and physical education. *European Physical Education Review* 3, 1, 58–67.

Health Promoting School Working Group (1996) *The Health Promoting School Award*. Ramsgate: Health Promoting School Working Group.

HEA (1998) *New Recommendations for Promoting Health-Enhancing Physical Activity with Young People (5–18 years)*. HEA.

Holland, J. (1995) 'An evaluation of a local health promoting school award scheme', unpublished MA dissertation. Canterbury Christ Church University College.

Jensen, B.B. (1992) *Environmental Health Education: Introduction and basic concepts*. Copenhagen: Research Centre for Environmental and Health Education, Royal Danish School of Educational Studies.

Parsons, C., Stears, D., Thomas, C., Thomas, L. and Holland, J. (1997) *The Implementation of the European Network of Health Promoting Schools in Different National*

Contexts.Canterbury: Centre for Health Education and Research, Canterbury Christ Church University College.

QCA (1999) *The Review of the National Curriculum in England: The consultation materials*. QCA: London.

World Health Organization (WHO) (1986) *Ottawa Charter for Health Promotion*. Copenhagen: WHO.

World Health Organization, Regional Office for Europe (1995) *The Overall Progress of the European Network of Health Promoting Schools Project, January–December 1994*. Copenhagen: WHO.

5 Curriculum Planning in Early Years Physical Education

Casting the Teacher in the Role of Researcher

Jes Woodhouse and Gill Bailey

Introduction

'Teachers are too often the servants of heads, advisers, researchers, textbooks, curriculum developers, examination boards or the Department for Education among others' (Hopkins 1993: 4). It does indeed seem like a very long time since teachers were required to jump through so many externally imposed hoops. Even though they are told repeatedly that such impositions are designed to raise standards of pupil achievement, there are many occasions when teachers become hard pressed to reconcile external demands with their knowledge and experience of teaching and learning (Kincheloe 1991). This is not to say that externally devised initiatives are necessarily 'bad' or ill informed. What seems to be the case is that the voice of the day-to-day practitioner is heeded all too rarely in the unrelenting drive to effect improvement in the quality of education in our schools.

Kincheloe (1991) suggests that the application to education of a western industrial organization model, with its bureaucratic, hierarchical structure, is to blame. The resulting view of teachers as 'blue collar workers, passive recipients of the dictates of the experts' (ibid.: vii) encourages a disregard of the special knowledge of those who actually do the everyday work. It has to be wondered if teachers themselves have become resigned to such a situation because, more than ever, they seem reluctant to make their voice heard in pedagogic debate. Perhaps the stuffing has been knocked out of them as supposedly objective evidence is repeatedly slanted to generate the image of a somewhat incompetent profession (*Times Educational Supplement* 1999). Little wonder that many members of the profession are feeling increasingly doubtful about the worth of their hard-won experience in informing decisions about teaching and learning.

One particular strategy that could help reverse this trend, and return a degree of professional autonomy to teachers, is for them to create more of their own educational knowledge to provide evidence to support their own pedagogic arguments. This would require teachers to incorporate research practices within their own teaching and for schools to become active research communities. Whilst there are many issues to be addressed with regard to such an extension of the teacher's role, there are clear advantages. 'Undertaking research into their own and colleagues' classrooms is one way teachers can take increased responsibility for their actions and create a more energetic and dynamic environment in which teaching and learning can occur' (Hopkins 1993: 1). It seems common sense that a community whose predominant role is to provide quality education should investigate systematically its practice as a means to improving or justifying that provision. Given that the vast majority of educational research to date has been conducted by 'outsiders' (Brause and Mayher 1991; Hopkins 1993; Kincheloe 1991) and given the view that little of that research has had any clear impact upon the improvement of practice (Brause and Mayher 1991; Gall et al. 1996; Hopkins 1993; Kallos 1980; Kincheloe 1991; Nisbet 1980; Robinson 1991; Walker 1985), a move to cast teachers and schools in the roles of researchers and research communities again seems timely. If one of the expressed purposes of educational research is to enable informed decisions to be made when looking to bring about improvements in practice, there is clearly a role for day-to-day practitioners in the process. By developing their own educational knowledge, teachers could move to a position of increased empowerment and accountability (Brause and Mayher 1991), liberate themselves from the control position they so often find themselves in (Hopkins 1993) and regain their voice within the forum of educational debate. This is not to suggest that teachers and schools be cast in the role of 'wreckers' of centralized policy, rather to locate them more actively in decisions surrounding the development and implementation of such policy. As Hopkins states: 'Successful implementation of any centralised innovation requires adaptation by teachers at the school level. It is not an either/or situation or a straight choice between 'top-down' or 'bottom-up' – it is a combination of both' (1993: 35). Casting the teacher in the role of researcher could assist greatly in the development of a more effective combination that reflects a shared commitment from all parties.

Whilst the concept of 'teacher as researcher' is not new, emanating as it did from the work of the Schools Council's Humanities Curriculum Project (1967–72) (Stenhouse 1975) and, whilst 'teachers making systematic inquiries into their own practice with a view to improving it' (Powney and Watts 1987: 3) is a growing trend, there is little to suggest widespread practice. Whilst good practice in teaching could be described as a continuous process of action research (Kincheloe 1991), it is rarely set up as such and, consequently, where it does exist, 'good teacher being action researcher' appears to be more of a covert than overt role.

The commonly held view of the researcher as someone who has to be objective and divorced from the situation being investigated, who has to spend inordinate amounts of time collecting and analysing data, has not prompted a headlong rush from teachers keen to take on the role. Indeed, given the immense pressures upon their time, the thought of having to take on yet another responsibility which, on the face of it, appears far removed from the role of the teacher, would not be something relished by the majority of teachers. However, it is not intended that teachers give up their teaching role to assume a research role; rather that teachers begin to apply systematic and empirical principles to critical reflection upon their craft with the aim of improving it (Hopkins 1993) and have the '"temerity" to investigate their own actions' (Powney and Watts 1993: 3). However, there will be a need to guard against this becoming yet another centralized demand, a demand that teachers become researchers and, even more disastrous, researchers of centrally imposed strategies to improve pupils' achievements in relation to centrally imposed standards (Elliot 1986, quoted in Kincheloe 1991).

Whilst there are clear advantages to teachers and schools incorporating research processes into their practice, there appears to be a number of issues to address before such a shift could become widespread. One of the major issues is that raised by Kincheloe, namely that too many teachers lack the pedagogical and relevant academic backgrounds required for them to integrate research processes into their work. A lack of clear understanding of the ideological, psychological and pedagogical assumptions that underlie their practice, and a lack of theoretical and analytical frames, mean that many teachers would, understandably, lack confidence in their ability to research practice. They would come to view it as yet something else to have to learn about and, to reiterate an earlier point, the immense pressures on them at present are not creating ideal conditions for the introduction and development of yet another initiative. Catch 22! Incorporating research into their practice could provide a key to relieving those pressures, but the pressures discourage such a seemingly large undertaking.

It was against this background that the small study informing this chapter was carried out.

The Research Context

It was during a discussion between the authors, one of whom was working in a primary school, that the seeds for a small-scale investigation into the practicability and worth of 'teacher as researcher' were sown. This discussion was centred upon proposed changes to the National Curriculum at Key Stages 1 and 2 during 1998 and, in particular, the options that were to be made available with regard to physical education. Whilst early years teachers have no statutory obligation to heed National Curriculum requirements, those whose reception classes are an integral part of a primary school (as was the case in this instance) are naturally mindful of the whole-school perspective. Consequently, they are aware of a responsibility to help the pupils in their classes develop in relation to their future, National-Curriculum-related experiences. With regard to physical education in the National Curriculum, those experiences, as they stood, would involve pupils at KS1 being taught dance, gymnastic activities and games (incorporated within each of which should be elements of the statutory General Requirements for Physical Education, related to positive attitudes, safe practice and healthy living), and, at KS2, these same activity areas along with athletic activities, outdoor and adventurous activities and swimming.

Whilst mindful of National Curriculum requirements, reception teachers are also conscious of best practice in early years education and are careful to ensure that the increasing focus on cognitive development, which seems to pervade all current initiatives at KS1 and KS2, does not cause them to compromise the accepted need to focus as much on the social, emotional and physical development of early years pupils. It was this desire to maintain a 'whole child' perspective when teaching physical education to reception class pupils that initiated the discussion.

The options available to KS1 and KS2 teachers were fourfold:

1   Prioritize – retain range of content in three areas of activity but emphasize performance.
2   Combine – combine teaching of skills common to dance and music.
3   Reduce – retain three areas of activity but reduce content in all or some.
4   Continue with existing requirements.

There is also mention of the key aspects drawn from the programme of study – positive attitudes, safe practice, and the planning/performing/evaluating – but the options given do not make clear the place of these key aspects in any modified curriculum plans. Indeed, if, within the prioritizing option, there is to be an emphasis on retaining content but emphasizing performance, how can the requirement for planning/performing/evaluating be met effectively?

On the face of it, Option 2 appeared to afford the greatest opportunity to preserve the essence of the existing experience. Whilst early years practice endeavours to combine experiences *across* the whole curriculum, there is also a tendency to combine activity areas *within* the physical education curriculum. A lesson may not be seen specifically as dance, games or gymnastics but as an opportunity to develop common skills in an environment which might at times be of a gymnastic, dance, games or, indeed, outdoor and adventurous nature. Whilst reflection on experience suggested that Option 2 was the most appropriate, it was thought that a decision based on research into existing practice, and its relation to the suggested options, would be that much better informed and that such a response would provide an opportunity to test the calls to cast the teacher in the role of researcher. It was also felt that a successful experience of such a role might provide the catalyst for other colleagues in the school to consider the possibilities of investigating their practice.

The initial response to this suggestion was not overly positive! The thought of having to take on a research role did not appeal for a number of reasons. Even though there was objective and subjective evidence to suggest that here was a committed, innovative and successful teacher who was not afraid to take on new initiatives, initial fears about lack of relevant experience and knowledge, increased workload, and distraction from the process of teaching were prominent. In addition, there was an understandable observation that research was the job of people from Schools of Education, along with a voiced concern that research hadn't done much to help teachers in the past. Such a response would probably be the norm rather than the exception amongst a majority of teachers and it brought home the vital need to be aware of these perceptions when broaching the subject.

With this in mind, it was clearly important that, if the teacher was to be cast as researcher in this instance, this first experience had to be a manageable one that could be incorporated into existing practice with minimum disruption and maximum effect. Hopkins (1993) suggests that, initially, teachers should only take on small-scale and relatively limited topics, as they are more liable to be completed satisfactorily in a short space of time and, therefore, prove to be reinforcing and encouraging. It was felt that this particular situation offered the opportunity to utilize a relatively simple research method to yield appropriate data. If it appeared too simplistic to be afforded the title of 'research' there was the powerful argument that if teachers are to be encouraged to adapt their existing role, it is important that the starting point is relevant to their experience and situation. Indeed, Walker (1985) suggests that setting the applied research enterprise in a professional context might lead to a somewhat less conventional view of 'research'. He feels that research by teachers may not have the conventional emphasis upon detailed knowledge of the literature or high levels of proficiency in the skills normally required by testing and survey research. As much as anything,

> to become expert in either of these areas demands more time, more training and more experience than most teachers are able to accumulate. What is required of teachers, of schools and of school systems is a range of other research skills, usually in relation to an immediate issue in one's own instruction.
>
> (Walker 1985: 3–4)

Against such a background, it appeared justifiable to ensure that this 'teacher as researcher' venture was as much to do with the teacher and the quality of her initial experience of the role as it was to do with the quality of the research.

There was one final point to consider before looking to set the research focus and select an appropriate method. This was the point raised earlier about teachers being lured into research that provides the autonomy to investigate their practice but remains within externally imposed bounds. In this instance, the teacher had agreed to use the research process to assist with decision-making, but the decision to be made was related to a set of externally imposed options. It had to be considered that the practice to be investigated might fail to match any of the suggested options and, if so, how would any resulting data be used?

Setting the Research Focus

The positive aspect of this venture was that the teacher had a question to which she was seeking an answer, and it was felt that some form of research could help towards the provision of an answer. It is obviously a more difficult situation if the teacher is being encouraged to research and, to facilitate such a move, she is almost forced to invent a topic to research. Quite often, it can be difficult for teachers to establish a precise focus for the enquiry (Hopkins 1993) but, whilst not necessarily required to set precise hypotheses, the teacher-researcher does need to be clear about the purposes of the research venture. Walker (1985) provides a number of examples of issues that the teacher might be required to focus upon and two of these were particularly pertinent to this case:

- the need to review alternative curriculum proposals and to judge their likely impact in practice
- the need to assess information coming into school from outside sources.

In this case, an outside source, the Qualification and Curriculum Authority (QCA), had proposed possible alternative approaches to the Physical Education curriculum at KS1 and KS2. Whilst the teacher's experience caused her to think that Option 2 provided the 'best fit' to existing practice, she was keen to investigate that practice to ascertain whether this was indeed the case. It was hoped that such an investigation would yield data to assist either in making a decision regarding the adoption of the most appropriate option or in questioning the suitability of the option available. Her work with reception children had a heavy emphasis upon the development of social skills, opportunities for which arose constantly. Whilst possible to anticipate the range of social skills which pupils could be enabled to develop during the reception year, and to be broadly proactive, assistance with the development of specific skills tended to be more of a reactive venture, taking place as and when most apt. With regard to physical education, the development of social skills is an integral feature, appearing as it does in the General Requirements for the subject. Indeed, physical education is a wonderful medium through which pupils can be enabled to develop physical, cognitive and emotional skills, as well as social skills. Whilst this is clearly desirable throughout the child's educational experience, it is very much the case during the early years and, for a long time, there has been an overt emphasis on the development of the 'whole child' during this phase of their formal education. Consequently, the teacher had to decide whether prioritization, combination, reduction or continuation provided a match to the ethos felt to be enshrined in her practice.

In addition to providing data to assist with curriculum-related decision-making, it was felt that this case should also be used to evaluate the manageability and worth of such research as perceived by a neophyte teacher-researcher.

Consequently, the following two sets of research questions emerged:

- When setting the learning focus for physical education lessons, how much consideration is given to physical, cognitive, social and emotional development?
- What is the range and frequency of activity areas used when teaching physical education?
- Is the nature of the physical education experience progressive in relation to the pupils' or the subject's development?
- Due to the prominent emphasis on socialization during this phase, how often does a response to the pupils' social behaviour impinge upon the planned learning focus?
- How does the nature of a series of physical education lessons match the suggested options for the revision of Physical Education in the National Curriculum?

- Did the research process help in making decisions about future curriculum planning in physical education?
- What impact, if any, did the research process have upon workload?
- Does a research emphasis cause the teacher to reflect any differently upon practice than might normally be the case?
- Given the experience, what are the teacher's thoughts about a more systematic approach to decision-making?

Deciding upon Research Method and Procedures

After identifying a focus for the research, and formulating related questions, the next task was to decide upon the method(s) and procedures best suited to the collection of relevant data. On the face of it, previous lesson plans and records of pupils' responses appeared to offer a logical source of data in respect of the majority of the curriculum-related questions. In this instance, however, such an obvious source of information was not readily available. The teacher was addressing these questions at the beginning of a new academic year and, at that stage, had no record of physical education work planned and executed with this particular group of children. In addition, lesson plans and evaluations for previous year groups had not been retained. Consequently, there was a need to create a means of gathering relevant data. In some ways this was an advantage in that any recording schedule and instrument could be designed specifically to reflect the purposes of the research, thereby ensuring a systematic focus upon the research questions when coming to record physical education lessons.

Having decided that a record of a series of physical education lessons could yield relevant data, an appropriate method of recording had to be found. Where the teacher is integrating the role of researcher into their existing role, and certainly in an instance like this where the experience was to be a new one, there appears to be a greater need to consider the practicability of any research method. Whilst methodological debate cannot be ignored, it is essential that some acceptable compromise is arrived at if the research is not to place an onerous burden upon the teacher. In saying this, practical considerations have to be taken into account by the majority of researchers. Perhaps the most important consideration is that the purposes of the research are not compromised detrimentally in the search for a manageable method.

In this instance, it was decided to design a recording sheet that could be completed relatively quickly whilst yielding data appropriate to the research questions. As it was the teacher who would have to use the sheet, she was involved fully in its design. To allow for a reliable amount of data, it was decided that this method of recording physical education lessons would be carried out over one school term and that a recording sheet would be completed as close as possible to the end of each physical education lesson. The accumulated data would then be analysed in relation to the specific, curriculum-related research questions.

With regard to the second set of research questions, it was decided that the teacher would answer the questions on what was essentially a questionnaire basis. However, the authors were very well known to each other and had collaborated previously on a number of educational initiatives. Consequently, it was felt appropriate for the teacher to use the second set of research questions to guide the report of her perceptions and her university-based collaborator would look to probe the responses if it was felt to be appropriate. It was important for the teacher to conduct as much of the data analysis and reporting as possible as both were aspects of the research process that had to be evaluated in terms of demands upon teacher time and expertise. However, she was provided with any advice and support she felt to be necessary during this initial venture.

The recording process began during the early weeks of the autumn term but, whilst it was planned to record throughout that term, a number of lessons were lost towards the end of the term due to inclement weather and seasonal demands on indoor hall space. Consequently, the recording process continued for the first half of the spring term.

Results from the Research

In total, 10 recording sheets were completed (Appendix 1). Here is a synopsis of the major features:

- No lesson was planned in relation to a specific 'area of activity'. The focus was much more upon generic skills that might later be applied in more specific contexts.
- The planned learning foci for the autumn term lessons were predominantly physical in nature; there was one mention of 'awareness of others' but this was as much a reference to spatial awareness as it was to social sensitivity. During the spring term there was an influx of new pupils and this resulted in a greater emphasis on safe practice and awareness, development of self-confidence and the expression of moods and feelings.

- Some lessons had a clear link to other areas of the curriculum i.e. music, English and drama.
- The planned learning focus was sometimes over-ridden as a reaction to events in lessons immediately prior to PE was felt to be more appropriate.
- Pupils' social behaviour rarely intruded on the planned learning focus to any disruptive degree. Any responses required from the teacher related to isolated incidents with individual children rather than a class problem. Over-excitement was the one feature that was mentioned on more than one occasion in relation to the whole class, and the teacher took the opportunity to help pupils to calm down and to listen. During the spring term, the larger group necessitated an increased focus on listening skills. This focus was linked to the development of movement skills in that pupils were encouraged to respond expressively in movement to various auditory stimuli.
- Any responses to individual or whole-class social-skill needs were effected within the lesson and/or taken through into immediate post-lesson time, sometimes becoming a focus for a few days after. They were rarely carried forward into the suggested learning focus for next week's PE lesson.
- During the autumn term the suggested learning focus for each subsequent PE lesson was predominantly physical. Occasionally there was mention of an accompanying social skill focus. During the spring term there was increased identification of social skills within the proposed learning focus.

These results enabled the following answers to be provided to the first set of research questions:

- When setting the learning focus for physical education lessons, how much consideration is given to physical, cognitive, social and emotional development?
  The focus for lessons ranged across physical, social and emotional development, although the focus on social and emotional became more pronounced after the influx of new pupils in the spring term.
- What is the range and frequency of activity areas used when teaching physical education?
  There were no specific references to the activity areas identified in the National Curriculum. It was possible to identify activities that could have been classified loosely as outdoor and adventurous, gymnastics, games and dance but the emphasis was more on generic, 'foundation' skills.
- Is the nature of the physical education experience progressive in relation to the pupils' or the subject's development?
  Progression was linked to the pupils' development. Learning activities were selected in response to the perceived needs of the pupils.
- Due to the prominent emphasis on socialization during this phase, how often does a response to the pupils' social behaviour impinge upon the planned learning focus?

During the lessons where a physical learning aim predominated there were instances where the pupils' social behaviour necessitated a shift away from that focus. However, the degree to which this took the focus away completely from the physical aspect was not great. During the spring term, where there was more of a social component to the learning focus, the social behaviour itself became a focus and was therefore an integral part of the lesson and the planned activities.

- How does the nature of a series of physical education lessons match the suggested options for the revision of physical education in the National Curriculum?

In this series of lessons, prioritizing the performing aspect of the subject would have affected negatively the opportunity to respond to social and emotional needs, whereas to retain three activity areas but reduce the content could have worked against the essentially outdoor and adventurous nature of one of the lessons. The option to combine common skills (within and across the curriculum) appeared to reflect more closely the teacher's practice. However, if the key aspects drawn from the programme of study are required to be incorporated, regardless of the option selected, the need during these lessons to respond to positive attitudes and safe practice could have been satisfied in that light.

As regards the second set of research questions, the teacher's responses were as follows:

- Did the research process help in making decisions about future curriculum planning in physical education?

Yes it did. It helped clarify earlier thoughts that the combining option was the closest one to existing practice. You think you know things from experience but the research process helped me to bring to the fore particular aspects of practice which I might not have considered in such depth. Mind you, it looks as though I could take up any of the options if I am required to include key aspects from the existing programme of study but I don't think reception children need to be doing specific activities so the combining option still looks like the best one.

- What impact, if any, did the research process have upon workload?

Anything new will have some impact. The recording did take time but it wasn't too excessive. I wasn't able to record directly after the lesson, but made sure that it was done by the end of that day at the latest. If researching in this way related to more lessons than one PE lesson a week I think it could become horrendous. It was funny that at the time we began the project David Blunkett told us that they were determined to reduce the amount of paperwork that teachers are required to do. I must say though that this was interesting paperwork which meant it was not as much of a burden. Normally paperwork is an added chore and, if I'm honest, PE was sometimes used as a pleasant interlude of sharing an enjoyable experience with the children, away from the normal pressures of the classroom-based paperwork. I have now come to realize more clearly the potential of PE, which I have lost by sometimes viewing it in this way. Of course, this now means I could be creating a lot more work for myself because I'll feel bound to take a more structured and thoughtful approach to the planning and teaching of PE.

- Did a research emphasis cause you to reflect any differently upon practice than might normally be the case?

  Yes. It brought to the fore the personal and social impacts on my practice and how, while proving it is normally a reactive process, I could be more systematic in planning such experiences. I could give more thought to the ways in which I group the children and the sorts of activities I could use to help them develop their social skills and personal coping skills. Doing the research really helped me to focus the mind more. I began to think a lot more about the opportunities to link to other areas of the curriculum. I am a sporty person and I enjoy doing PE with the children but I can see how there is much more I could be doing in an area that they enjoy so much. Also, while I've always talked about my practice with other members of staff in the staffroom, this process made me record my practice and this could be used to help not only me but other members of staff. By having a record of what happened, it could make it easier to share with more members of staff. I think it is also a good thing to have some written evidence to help support and justify decisions and, by having a record of what happened, it could make it easier to provide documented information to other members of staff.

- Given the experience, what are your thoughts about adopting a more systematic approach to decision-making?

  I do feel I should be more systematic because it creates a much clearer focus for learning and teaching, certainly on longer-term issues. I can't help but think though that this research supported my initial feeling about which option to take and I wonder how many of our hunches, which come out of experience, are actually informed hunches. That experience is our research I think, but obviously it isn't as thorough as the research process. It certainly brought to light factors which I might not normally have considered but I'm still hesitant because of a worry about extra work. It is a good idea but I'm doing so much as it is and if I can make decisions without the extra work, and if those decisions are okay, which they seem to be, that is much more appealing. But we do need more teachers' views in the decision-making process to get a healthy debate, a bigger picture, and supporting evidence for those teachers would obviously add more clout to their views. I think it is something of a difficult position, I can see the benefit, but I'm worried about the seeming threat of a lot more work. To do research properly it needs to be thorough if it is to hold weight and I still think we've got so many other pressures on that it would be hard to do it properly. This project was very small but I still feel I should have put more into it, but I didn't feel I had the time. I mean, proper research would take so much time wouldn't it? It is difficult, because this process could help me to focus at a time when there seems to be so much going on, but because there is so much going on, it becomes hard to focus on something like this. Perhaps researchers should work more closely with teachers because that is their job and they could help a lot.

Issues Arising from Results

The overarching focus of the project was to assess the manageability and worth of casting the teacher in the role of researcher. The teacher's responses to the second set of research questions go a long way to providing this assessment and the main issue arising appears centred upon the perceived trade off between manageability and worth. The process was seen to be valuable and interesting, providing the teacher with a much clearer insight into her practice. The repeated use of terms such as 'focus', 'clarify' and 'bring to light' support this. Opposing this benefit is the repeated concern about increased workload. Whilst it is possible to view the recording process employed as a relatively small extension to normal planning and evaluating procedures, the concern about research involving anything beyond this simple process, or indeed, carrying out such a process over a longer time, was obvious.

It could be that preconceived notions about the nature of research contributed to a perception of the task as something more onerous than it was. However, personal perceptions deserve great consideration when attempting to encourage individuals into new ventures. If an individual perceives research as a time-consuming, very thorough process, normally conducted by research 'experts', any request for them to incorporate research into their practice may set alarm bells ringing. However, the teacher's comment about her experiences leading to informed hunches reflects the existence of a foundation for research. Reflective practitioners may well be engaging in a form of on-going research that informs much of what they do. It may lack the theoretical frameworks, thoroughness and systematic approaches that many would associate with 'proper' research, but good practitioners can often be seen to be looking for or testing hypotheses related to effective teaching and learning. What they may not be doing is recording those efforts in any formal fashion and it is this lack of hard evidence that prevents them from putting forward their experiences as contributions to educational debate. However, the recording of their practice in a more formalized fashion could be the aspect of the research process that would fuel concern about increased workload.

In many ways, good teaching integrates a form of research in that it seeks to resolve numerous pedagogical problems on a daily basis. It seems sensible, therefore, to take this feature of good practice and demonstrate to teachers how such a process can make a valuable contribution to the development of new educational knowledge. What may well be required, though, is a means of helping them record their endeavours on this front.

It cannot be forgotten that the concerns over innumerable pressures, voiced by the teacher in this small study, are not uncommon across the profession. Whilst she enjoyed the research process and the light it shed on a number of issues, the teacher in this study could not help but return to the fact that 'there is so much else going on'. Regardless of any potential benefit, casting the teacher in the role of researcher or, perhaps more accurately, encouraging teachers to integrate features of the research process into their practice, is a venture that requires a deal of sensitivity to these pressures. And who will encourage and support such a venture?

It seems logical for Schools of Education to endeavour to establish and nurture research networks within local schools. However, unless some of the members of those Schools of Education are truly empathetic to the situation currently affecting teachers, this could prove to be the straw that breaks the camel's back rather than the straw required to make the building bricks for a stronger, school-originated contribution to educational debate.

Such empathy would clearly be a requirement if 'teacher as researcher' were a role to be imposed upon all teachers. However, teachers are currently free to choose whether to take on such a role and, in the light of the comments made by the teacher in this study, those who are motivated to do so can benefit greatly on a number of fronts. Clearly, there will be a need to appreciate some of the practical constraints, the bulk of which appear to relate to the recording of data. However, if the teacher is able to devote some initial time to a review of the numerous research methods available, he or she may be able to select methods that can be incorporated readily into recording and evaluation procedures that already exist in relation to their teaching. There is little doubt that a clear focus for the research will help the teacher manage any project more effectively. In addition, if that focus is on a practice-related decision to be made or problem to be solved, the motivation to research should be maintained more easily. For the neophyte teacher-researcher, who may be a little unsure of the best way to tackle an initial project, there is nothing to be lost by contacting the School of Education at their local Higher Education establishment, where help might be at hand.

Summary

This small study showed that, when looking to make curriculum-planning decisions, a teacher can benefit from engaging in the research process. Undoubtedly, the teacher who is motivated to engage in research as an integral part of practice will benefit greatly on a number of fronts. However, whilst good teaching may include aspects of this process, many teachers may well have a preconceived notion of research which posits it as yet another bolt-on rather than something integral to practice. Although the benefits to them of accumulating evidence to support and justify their decisions and practices are clear, some thought must be given to the ways in which they can be helped to subsume such practice into their existing work. If this is not done, there is the danger that teachers will continue to be the subjects of other people's research and, consequently, continue to have a very limited voice in the wider educational forum. In this instance, the teacher was provided with support, encouragement and advice throughout the process yet still came out of it with concerns about any longer-term or larger commitment. This is not to sound defeatist, rather to provide a realistic picture of a committed, conscientious teacher who would love to spend more time investigating her practice, if only there weren't so many other things going on. The challenge to those who would seek to help teachers liberate themselves from a constant stream of 'other things going on' is to ensure that they themselves do not become another example of the same. However, the teacher who is motivated to incorporate research into their practice should draw further inspiration from the results of this study. As long as some of the practical hurdles are appreciated and approached positively, there is much to be gained, not least of which might be the evidence required to help re-establish the voice of teachers in the wider forum of educational debate.

References

Brause, R.S. and Mahyer, J.S. (eds) (1991) *Search and Research: What the enquiring teacher needs to know.* London: Falmer.

Gall, M.D., Borg, W.R., and Gall, J.P. (1996) *Educational Research - An Introduction,* 6th edn. White Plains, NY: Longman.

Hopkins, D. (1993) *A Teacher's Guide to Classroom Research* 2nd edn. Buckingham: Open University Press.

Kallos, D. (1980) 'On educational phenomena and educational research', in W.B. Dockrell and D. Hamilton (eds) (1980) *Rethinking Educational Research.* London: Hodder & Stoughton.

Kincheloe, J.L. (1991) *Teachers as Researchers: Qualitative inquiry as a path to empowerment.* London: Falmer.

Nisbet, J. (1980) 'Educational research: the state of the art', in W.B. Dockrell and D. Hamilton (eds) (1980) *Rethinking Educational Research.* London: Hodder & Stoughton.

Powney, J., and Watts, M. (1987) *Interviewing in Educational Research.* London: Routledge & Kegan Paul.

Robinson, V. (1991) *Problem-Based Methodology: Research for the improvement of practice.* Oxford: Pergamon.

Stenhouse, L. (1975) *An Introduction to Curriculum Research and Development.* London: Heinemann.

Times Educational Supplement (1999) 'Point to paranoia' (editorial), no. 4314, 5 March.

Walker, R. (1985) *Doing Research: A handbook for teachers.* London: Routledge.

Appendix 1

Physical Education

Lesson No. 1

Activity Area   *School grounds*

Date   *10.9.98*

Planned Learning Focus
Awareness of space and others
Moving around as a group (large)

Reason(s) for this Focus
Children are new to the school – introduction to the school grounds

---

During the lesson, did pupils' behaviour demand a response removed from this learning focus?

Whole group

Specific group

Individual pupils
Some individuals intruded on others' space

Did you respond within the lesson? If so how?
Yes, by explaining how they should move in a large group – be aware of others

---

Will it affect the learning focus for the next PE lesson or did you respond in the lesson immediately following PE?
Will probably need to revise this message often in lessons and at other times out of lessons and in PE

Suggested learning focus for next PE lesson
Finding spaces on their own

Physical Education   Lesson No. 2

Activity Area   *School hall*   Date   *17.9.98*

Planned Learning Focus
Positional language + finding spaces (continued focus on awareness of space and others)

Reason(s) for this Focus
It is the first time in the school hall for some children

During the lesson, did pupils' behaviour demand a response removed from this learning focus?
No not really

Whole group
Were rather excitable and understandably noisy

Specific group

Individual pupils

Did you respond within the lesson? If so how?
Yes – had a quiet time – tip-toe from space to space, move slowly to a corner, lie as still as a mouse in the centre of the hall, etc.

Will it affect the learning focus for the next PE lesson or did you respond in the lesson immediately following PE?

Suggested learning focus for next PE lesson
Moving with increasing control and co-ordination (run, walk, skip, hop, etc.)

Physical Education

Lesson No. 3

Activity Area   *School field*

Date   *24.9.98*

Planned Learning Focus
Had planned to use hall for the suggested learning focus of last lesson but weather was so good I decided to go outside

warm-up of follow my leader – walk, run, jump, hop, skip
Main focus was ball skills – send, receive and travel with

Reason(s) for this Focus

During the lesson, did pupils' behaviour demand a response removed from this learning focus?
No each child was focused for most of the lesson

Whole group

Specific group

Individual pupils
One child sat down and did not want to play because her friend would not partner her

Did you respond within the lesson? If so how?
Yes – I became her partner

Will it affect the learning focus for the next PE lesson or did you respond in the lesson immediately following PE?
Discussed friendships at a later time during the week – how it is important to be friendly with more than one person

Suggested learning focus for next PE lesson
(continue this week's skills)
Working with others (use Huggy Bears as a warm up)

Physical Education   Lesson No. 4

Activity Area   *School hall*   Date   *8.10.98*

Planned Learning Focus
Had planned to continue with ball skills but changed to performing actions in response to a stimulus

---

Reason(s) for this Focus
A child brought in a book from home which we had read in class and because the children enjoyed it so much, I decided to use it for PE. 'We're going on a Bear Hunt' by Michael Rosen

---

During the lesson, did pupils' behaviour demand a response removed from this learning focus?

Whole group
Very focused but excitable

Specific group

Individual pupils

Did you respond within the lesson? If so how?
Yes, praised those who remained on task

Will it affect the learning focus for the next PE lesson or did you respond in the lesson immediately following PE?
Not particularly though I will begin the lesson explaining that I expect them to listen to instructions or to the stimulus if there is one

---

Suggested learning focus for next PE lesson
Moving confidently and imaginatively (as it is 'Book Week' – perhaps another story book)

Physical Education   Lesson No. 5

Activity Area   *School hall*   Date   *15.10.98*

Planned Learning Focus
Move confidently and imaginatively (increasing control and co-ordination)

Reason(s) for this Focus
Linking to drama through the use of a story as a stimulus – this week is 'Book Week'

During the lesson, did pupils' behaviour demand a response removed from this learning focus?

Whole group

Specific group

Individual pupils
Over-excitable, unable to control their own excitement – therefore not concentrating on next task. Plus some children had ideas of their own to add to the story

---

Did you respond within the lesson? If so how?
Yes – getting attention of 'the whole class' before moving on the the next part of the story.

Plus listening (as a class) to individuals' ideas, putting some into action (retaining others for the next lesson through lack of time)

Will it affect the learning focus for the next PE lesson or did you respond in the lesson immediately following PE?
The intention was to carry on this lesson next week – 'tuning' the movements encountered this week – will add in ideas of individuals. Asking them to lead a part of the session

---

Suggested learning focus for next PE lesson
As this week – increasing children's confidence and imagination, hopefully

Physical Education	Lesson No. 6
Activity Area *School hall*	Date *22.10.98*

Planned Learning Focus
To move confidently and imaginatively – with an awareness of others

Reason(s) for this Focus
Continuation of last week's session – refining their movements and working with others

During the lesson, did pupils' behaviour demand a response removed from this learning focus?
No, they were very focused this week, just a small hiccup when I asked them to arrange themselves into groups

Whole group

Specific group

Individual pupils
2 individuals had problems with this
1 not knowing which group to go to through shyness – not a confident child within the class (1 female)
1 wanting others to join her (female)

Did you respond within the lesson? If so how?
Yes, by suggesting which groups they should join and encouraging those groups to accept them

Will it affect the learning focus for the next PE lesson or did you respond in the lesson immediately following PE?
These were social issues which will be looked at throughout the school day – wherever group dynamics come into play

Suggested learning focus for next PE lesson

Physical Education

Lesson No. 7

Activity Area   *School hall*

Date   *4.11.98*

Class Topic – Stories: Mr Rush/Mr Slow

Planned Learning Focus
Awareness of space and using it safely

Reason(s) for this Focus
Class size has doubled
Introducing new intake of children to PE session

During the lesson, did pupils' behaviour demand a response removed from this learning focus?

Whole group
Listening skills need to be worked on

Specific group

Individual pupils
Children that are lacking in confidence needed an adult or 'a friend' to be close to them to encourage them to 'move'

Did you respond within the lesson? If so how?
Yes, for new shy children, I held their hand or gave them 'a friend' to hold their hands and show them what they could do

---

Will it affect the learning focus for the next PE lesson or did you respond in the lesson immediately following PE?
Will continue with the learning focus. 'Shy' children will need 'a friend' until they feel confident to work on their own

---

Suggested learning focus for next PE lesson
Responding to teacher's voice (listening carefully)
Use space safely

Physical Education	Lesson No. 8
Activity Area *School hall*	Date *18.1.99*

Class Topic – Stories/Made up story about assortment of Mr Men

---

Planned Learning Focus
Respond in movement to teacher's voice, expressing moods and feelings
To use space safely

Reason(s) for this Focus
Encourage children to listen carefully to instructions/teacher's voice
Using this session to assess Personal and Social aspect of Baseline Assessment for the new intake

---

During the lesson, did pupils' behaviour demand a response removed from this learning focus?
No they were focused generally as a group

Whole group

Specific group

Individual pupils
3 children still needed a friend to help them but the remainder of the new intake integrated well into the activity. Good response to the activity

---

Did you respond within the lesson? If so how?
Yes. I gave encouragement and praise to the whole group and more specifically to those who needed it most

---

Will it affect the learning focus for the next PE lesson or did you respond in the lesson immediately following PE?
We have been looking specifically at 'listening skills' in the classroom. I will continue to do this throughout the next week in the classroom and in the hall. All but 3 enjoyed the activity

---

Suggested learning focus for next PE lesson
Responding to another stimulus

Physical Education

Lesson No. 9

Activity Area

Date   *25.1.99*

Class Topic – Stories/The 3 Billy Goats Gruff

Planned Learning Focus
Respond in movement to percussion – expressing moods and feelings

Reason(s) for this Focus
To encourage listening. Moving to a variety of percussion instruments to express moods and feelings. We are looking at this in class too as part of Personal and Social Development

---

During the lesson, did pupils' behaviour demand a response removed from this learning focus?

Whole group

Specific group

Individual pupils
Some children needed encouragement from an adult and/or their friends

---

Did you respond within the lesson? If so how?
Yes through praise and encouragement

Will it affect the learning focus for the next PE lesson or did you respond in the lesson immediately following PE?
Not really

Suggested learning focus for next PE lesson
Respond in movement to a music stimulus

Physical Education   Lesson No. 10

Activity Area   Date   *1.2.99*

Class Topic – Peter and the Wolf

Planned Learning Focus
Respond in movement to music – expressing moods and feelings

Reason(s) for this Focus

We have been looking at this story (Peter and the Wolf) in class and have been discussing feelings

---

During the lesson, did pupils' behaviour demand a response removed from this learning focus?

Whole group

Specific group

Individual pupils
One or two children became very involved in playing their parts – especially the wolf

---

Did you respond within the lesson? If so how?
Yes by reminding the group about using space safely

Will it affect the learning focus for the next PE lesson or did you respond in the lesson immediately following PE?
No

Suggested learning focus for next PE lesson
Continue with this story but shifting the focus to more specific movement (high/low, fast/slow, heavy/light)

6 Safe Practice in Primary School Physical Education

Carole Raymond

This chapter will examine the concept of safe practice in physical education and how teachers can make use of current research evidence to inform and improve their own practice in the primary school.

Safe practice attracts attention from various disciplines. For example, sports psychologists are increasingly interested in the impact of burnout and the effect of goal-setting and stress management to reduce accidents in sport; lawyers are interested in compensating students for injuries incurred in school accidents. Those involved in education management tend to focus on how they can make the school environment a safer place and physical education specialists tend to extend this to the maintenance of specialist facilities and equipment. This chapter can therefore only give a brief overview of selected issues and as such will address those aspects specifically relevant to safe practice in primary school physical education. It is written for the reflective practitioner involved in teaching classroom physical education or for those with specific responsibility for the management of health and safety such as the subject leader. In one of the opening sections I will provide a snapshot of one of my own experiences that inevitably shaped my outlook. In doing this I hope readers will understand how this experience has informed my own practice and research. Before any discussion of safe practice can proceed it seems reasonable to have some shared understanding of what safe practice actually means. An overview of relevant research that relates to safe practice and the implications of this research will follow this.

Background

In a short paper in the *Sports Teacher* in 1988 I recalled a personal experience which raised my awareness of how easy it is for an accident to happen and how such an experience can have a life-long impact not only on the injured person but all those involved. As a Duke of Edinburgh Award candidate in the mid-1960s, I assisted three experienced staff on a children's holiday project. It was a residential experience for young people, aged 8–12 years, who had problems at home or who were unlikely to get a holiday. It was a summer evening and the children had had a hectic day swimming, playing games in the gym and on the field. It was time to put away the equipment and move indoors for cartoons, quizzes and prize bingo! I can remember one of the teachers settling the children down and checking that they were all in and seated. There were three missing and so another member of staff quickly went out to the field to call them in. I followed. Just as she turned the corner another member of staff appeared out of the hostel block and they simultaneously bellowed to the three children still playing on the field. As this happened one of the boys lifted the golf club in his hand and swung it forward. There was a scream. The teachers ran towards the boys and saw that one of them had been hit in the eye. The boy was rushed to hospital where the wound was diagnosed as serious and his parents were called. His eye suffered permanent damage and loss of sight.

When the teacher returned from the hospital early the next day everyone appeared in a state of shock. Many questions were asked: 'Why were the boys still on the field?', 'They had only just been called ... and the children know that they must not stay out on their own ...'. Teachers questioned their own level of supervision: was it appropriate? 'We've done this every night and nothing like this has happened before'. The accident was recorded in the centre's report book and the official paperwork completed and returned to the LEA office. The holiday continued, as did the searching questions. The experience has stayed with me throughout my work as a teacher and teacher educator.

In this instance the parents were very supportive of the staff and accepted the level of care provided. They knew their son very well and were aware of his tendency to disregard instructions. At the time there was no threat of legal action. I have often recalled this incident to colleagues and students, and each time I recall what I learned from the experience and how it shaped my own practice. The staff was very experienced and dealt with the situation in a very calm and professional manner. They were familiar with accident and emergency procedures. It made me realize that parents have an expectation of teachers and that this expectation can be reasonable. Nevertheless there was clearly the potential for conflict, as many questions were asked about how and why the accident happened. It made me appreciate that in reality accidents can and do happen despite good supervision, established routines and high standards of pupil discipline. It also constantly reminds me of how accidents can be very frightening experiences and that to learn from our experiences, and those of others, is crucial to teachers' ongoing professional development.

It is now 30 years on and I would like to think that should a similar tragedy occur today the parents' confidence in the staff and the level of care they had taken would be the same − after all, it was an accident. But I doubt it very much. Even if parents were supportive of the staff times have changed. There could be the bombshell of 'alleged negligence' and the pursuit of damages, since compensation could make the child's life more comfortable. This is because British society has become more safety-conscious and public services, including education, have faced increasing Health and Safety regulation. This serves to ensure those employed in education, and pupils, who may be affected by education provision, are protected. Failure to undertake these responsibilities can lead to prosecution. More importantly, however, failure to meet regulations may lead to accident and personal injury that can have a severe impact on an individual's life. During the last decade the reporting of various tragedies involving pupils of different ages has raised British society's awareness of safety and influenced public attitudes towards litigation.

Add to this the unprecedented efforts to initiate change in British schools (Education Reform Act (ERA) 1988) and its impact on the way teachers work. Most significantly this has involved prescriptions from policy-makers leading to changes in the way teachers are trained, the curriculum available to pupils and how it should be taught, league tables of performance and teacher appraisal. The teaching profession has found itself confronted by the need to address its practices as they relate to improving standards, assuring quality and demonstrating effectiveness. All of this reflects an emphasis on school effectiveness and improvement dominated by a mechanistic performance management approach. Such an approach has been previously associated with commercial management where consumers have rights and to which the full rigours of law as a primary form of regulation are inevitable. This consumer culture has permeated education and pupils and their parents are increasingly seen as 'clients' with 'consumer rights'. Litigation has become big business. Hence a change in parents' attitudes to look to blame someone if their child is involved in an accident at school and the need for schools to look more closely at the management of safe practice in physical education.

Safe Practice – What Does it Mean?

I believe safety and safe practice has an intellectual worth although it can often be difficult to convince others of this. Instead, many see 'accident prevention' or 'negligence avoidance' as the main motive for safe practice. Whilst I cannot disagree that these are desirable outcomes, safety and safe practice in physical education is much more. It is inevitable that accidents will happen: after all physical education, by its very nature, has an element of risk, challenge and adventure. Providing a safe environment does not mean simply removing that risk (often referred to as the negligence avoidance strategy whereby teachers simply remove any activity involving risk). Is this what the future holds for physical education? Although accidents will occur because they cannot always be foreseen, teachers have a legal duty to work within a system which demonstrates a realistic use of methods and which successfully anticipates and eliminates foreseeable risk (BAALPE 1995: 21) Being able to do this involves teachers adopting a strategy known as safety management. It is about creating an effective learning environment where children are set tasks that expose them to risk and challenge in a systematic way. It means that any risk is managed. Whilst safety has always been a top priority for teachers, more and more

93

teachers must recognize that they are also educators in the law arena and that they not only need to protect children but also their own professional integrity.

It is interesting to note that few studies on effective teaching and learning actually make reference to safe practice (see Siedentop 1989; Silverman 1991). Metzler, a respected worker in the field of teacher effectiveness in physical education provided a list of effective teacher/learner process indicators for PE (1990: 61). This work acknowledged the need for the establishment of a safe learning environment yet recognized that there was little empirical support for its role in effective teaching, suggesting that it ought to be a necessary precondition for teaching many activities in PE. This view is shared by the British Association of Advisers and Lecturers in Physical Education (BAALPE), who state that safe practice should be an integral feature of all aspects and in all phases of education (1995, 7). They expand this in relation to physical education concluding that safe practice has two components. The first embraces the responsibilities of the teacher and the second is concerned with the process of education.

Responsibilities of the Teacher

Teachers' legal responsibilities are outlined in a number of documents. Under the Health and Safety at Work (HSW) Act (1974) they have a duty to comply with any safety instructions given to them by their employer, i.e. the education authority in the case of maintained schools and the governors in the case of independent schools. Section 2(3) of the Act places a duty of care on every employer (LEA) to prepare, and, as often as appropriate to revise, a written statement on general policy in respect of the health and safety of employees and the organization and arrangements for carrying out that policy. The employers must bring this to the attention of their employees (teachers). This also applies to safe premises and safe environment in which employees and pupils will work. Failure to do can result in prosecution.

It may well be the case that the employer's advice is more restrictive than that given in additional guidance or literature, for example it may ban the use of certain equipment such as trampettes or curtail such activities as diving during swimming lessons or outdoor and adventurous activities off site. In this case, the teachers have a legal duty to follow the employer's instructions. However, it is worth noting that teachers are perfectly at liberty to challenge the reasoning behind the employer's instructions and seek to get the local regulations modified.

As well as the HSW Act, the Management of Health and Safety at Work 1992 regulations set down the revised guidelines that require all employers to introduce measures for planning, organizing, monitoring and reviewing their arrangements for the management of health and safety. This is known as risk assessment and is all about controlling potential hazards. This means that governing bodies and their headteachers must identify and assess the levels of risk that exist in curriculum activities, and ensure the design and implemention of effective risk control measures, appropriate systems, procedures and policies to manage, control and protect these measures and to develop them through adequate health and safety training.

In addition to their statutory duties, heads and teachers have a common law *duty of care* for pupils, which relates to the long-established position of teachers *in loco parentis*. The law requires that teachers must exercise the same standard of care that a reasonable parent would exercise. It is worth noting that both parents and the general public often set the professional responsibility for children's well being and safety much higher than that normally expected of a parent: they assume that teachers will be more aware of the potential dangers to pupils.

The law also expects that all teachers will work within a *modus operandi* that identifies all the foreseeable safety problems associated with the activities undertaken in relation to the curriculum (BAALPE 1995: 21). In this sense safe practice means that 'Over the years, teachers have established and regularly used teaching practices and procedures which have reliably avoided foreseeable accidents without reducing the challenge and developmental value of physical education for young people' (23).

This is summarized as 'regular and approved practice'. All of this applies to the school curriculum and extra-curricular activities, whether undertaken on or away from the school site. When involved in residential visits the duty of care applies 24 hours a day. Any breach of these duties that cause injury or loss may give rise to a claim for damages (compensation) or sometimes even to criminal penalties.

Teachers' professional responsibilities are also well documented under the *Teachers' Pay and Conditions Document*, published annually, which sets out a teacher's professional duties such as 'maintaining good order and discipline among the pupils and safeguarding their health and safety both when they are authorised to be on the school premises and when they are engaged in authorised activities elsewhere' (DfE 1995, par. 35).

More recently specific responsibilities related to health and safety are stipulated in the 'Standards for Newly Qualified Teachers' (DfEE 1998: 10). Similarly, the *National Standards for Subject Leaders* (TTA 1998) identifies specific expectations that subject leaders should know about and understand: 'the characteristics of high quality teaching in the subject and the main strategies for improving and sustaining high standards of teaching, learning and achievement of all pupils; ... health and safety requirements, including where to obtain expert advice' (6).

The exemplification of these standards in physical education is outlined by BAALPE in *Achieving Excellence as a Subject Leader in Physical Education*. It suggests that physical education leaders should adhere to school Health and Safety policy and advice, using BAALPE safety guidance documents for information and direction. They should also provide department health and safety policy, the development of which can be approached in two ways; first, by

updated and monitored advice from education and training
d second, by establishing a systematic approach to safety in
y in relation to equipment, facilities and teaching both on- and
y, physical education subject leaders should ensure the existence
risk assessments and procedures and, by providing training, ensure
rst aid training and an understanding of the process of risk assess-
l staff. In addition, pupils should be encouraged to take personal
responsibility for hygiene and safety (1998: 13). Furthermore, the TTA suggests
that research and inspection evidence demonstrates the close correlation
between the quality of teaching and the achievement of pupils and between the
quality of leadership and the quality of teaching (1998: 1).

Process of Education

No one would disagree that teachers clearly need to teach safely and it is
reasonable to assume that teachers are very conscious of the need for creating a
safe environment. But they also have a responsibility for teaching safety and
this involves providing opportunities for young people to develop the knowledge, skills and understanding of safety principles as applied to themselves and
others. This has become more prescriptive since the introduction of the
National Curriculum in Physical Education (NCPE), which stipulated that
children should be taught to:

> be concerned with their own safety and that of others' in all activities
> undertaken;
> lift, carry and place equipment safely;
> understand why particular clothing, footwear and protection are worn for
> different activities;
> understand the safety risks of wearing inappropriate clothing, footwear and
> jewellery;
> respond readily to instructions and signals within established routines, and
> follow relevant rules and codes.
>
> (DES 1992: 3)

Whilst this Order has been subsequently revised, aspects of teaching safety
remain on the agenda (see DfE 1995). It is important, therefore, to recognize
that teachers need to plan intentional experiences in order for children to
develop the appropriate knowledge, skills and understanding to carry forward
into other aspects of their life. The development of such skills cannot be left to
chance (Croner 1998) and it is important for teachers to be literate regarding
their legal and professional responsibilities. In addition to this, when they are
talking about safe practice teachers must be aware of a process which, at face
value at least, has been variously described as a cycle of phases or moments.
These include thinking, acting, monitoring and reflecting.

How can Teachers Make Use of Research Evidence to Promote Safe Practice?

Although recent research on health and fitness (see Chapter 3), multi-cultural issues (see Chapter 8) and gender (see Chapter 7) in physical education can help teachers make more informed decisions about their own teaching there is very little specific research reported on safe practice. Perhaps this is because 'safety' is implicit in much of the research into pedagogical aspects of physical education, not only aspects of how teachers teach, but how pupils learn.

It is tremendously important to stay abreast of professional issues and problems which may affect the way teachers work. Many concerns about safety are raised at school level during staff-room discussions and staff meetings and they may feature as aspects of continuing professional development opportunities. It is very unlikely that the classroom teacher will have the opportunity to search through legal documents, read case study materials or gain access to a broad spectrum of journals, both research and professional, in order to glean ideas for improving the learning environment. But there is a need to up-date functional knowledge of the teacher's responsibilities and how they manifest themselves in practice. Ignorance may be bliss, but it may not help schools refute charges of negligence and it can lead to an impoverished curriculum for young people.

As was mentioned in Chapter 1, different types of research can inform practice. Whilst there have been few in-depth empirical studies conducted there are a number of different methods being employed to monitor and assess what accidents happen and why.

Surveys on accidents in schools have revealed that schools are generally safe places. However, statistics collated by the Health and Safety Executive (HSE), presented at a joint seminar between BAALPE and HSE, reveal that of all the school accidents reported in 1995–6 the highest percentage were in sport (Figure 6.1). Such statistical surveys not only provide data to shape our understanding of a national picture of the number of accidents to young people in schools, but begin to suggest differences in pupils' age, the type of school (primary and secondary), and the range of settings and activity type (see Figures 6.2, 6.3, 6.4 and 6.5). For example young people between the ages of 8 and 14 years old are more prone to accidents than any other age group. Additionally, statistics suggest that more accidents happen on the playing fields and in gymnastics (Figure 6.2) and this may suggest a need for more information to say why this happens and what the profession can do to maintain the challenge of the different environments but limit the number of accidents.

Many LEA health and safety officers also collect this type of survey data. Under RIDDOR (1995) (The Reporting of Injuries, Disease and Dangerous Occurrences Regulations) schools are now required to report to the LEA, who in turn report to the Health and Safety Executive, any death or major injury. The latter includes fractures (other than to feet and hands) and any unconsciousness. This has to be done by telephone and in writing within seven days. Some schools also examine their own accident report books in order to look for

97

Figure 6.1   Injuries to School Pupils 1995–6

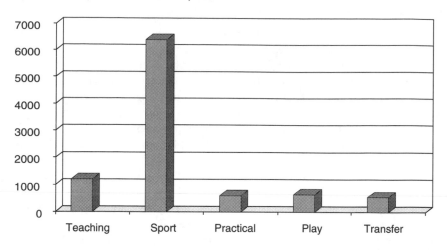

Figure 6.2   Injuries to School Pupils Arising from Sports Activities 1991/2–1995/6

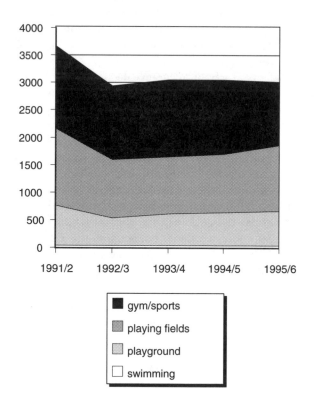

Figure 6.3 Injuries to School Pupils During Swimming Activities 1996/7

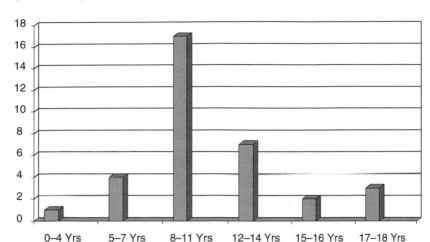

Figure 6.4 Injuries to School Pupils During Sports Activities on Playing Fields 1996/7

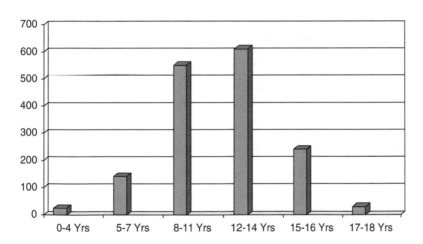

any common incidents or patterns of injury that may influence their safety policy or risk assessments.

Whilst much can be learned from statistics much more can be gained from an examination of case-study reports, which can help us to understand why accidents happen. By analysing accidents in reality and not hypothetical situations teachers can learn from the experiences and mistakes of others. For example:

When working on an experiment a pupil scalded himself ...

99

A young lad designing a ... slipped when using the scissors and cut himself badly ...

A young girl fell from the wall bars while climbing during a gymnastics lesson; she broke her ankle ...

A pupil slipped on wet leaves on the playground and badly damaged her knee ...

A young lad fell, caught his foot in a hole on the playing field and broke his ankle ...

None of these sound unusual accidents but they do have one thing in common: the LEA was sued for damages and was shown to be liable for the injuries due to negligence. An analysis of such cases reveals a sad fact that many of these accidents and the resulting litigation could have been prevented if the teacher in charge had taken due care as recognized in codes of regular and approved practice.

Using a case study approach, Thomas (1994) examined the detailed reports on relatively recent tragedies and incidents that have occurred whilst pupils were engaged in authorized school activities.[1] Despite differences in pupils' ages, the types of school, range of settings and activity types, her findings revealed that there are a number of similarities contributing to why accidents happen. She suggested that these pivot around five themes:

1 Bad luck – factors outside of the teachers' control;
2 Poor decision-making and subsequent reaction to the situation;

Figure 6.5 Injuries to School Pupils During Activities in Gymnasia 1996/7

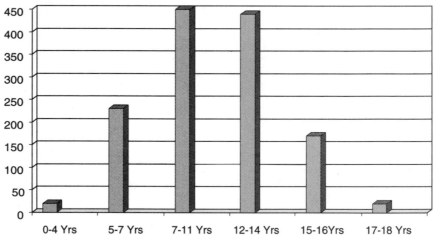

3   Lack of adequate and appropriate group management, supervision and orga-
    nization;
4   Over-estimation of (a) the teacher's ability – knowledge, understanding
    and competence – and (b) the pupil's sense of responsibility;
5   Under-estimation of potential risk and hazard.

Any one or combination of these factors may contribute to why an accident might
happen. This type of work helps us to realize that accidents cannot always be
predicted and that they happen due to one or a number of reasons. We must also
recognize that no amount of planning can guarantee that school experiences will
be incident-free. What is important is that we know about those factors that may
lead to accidents over which we have some control and are sure to adopt suitable
practice to eliminate any foreseeable risk. A good example of this level of analysis
and how it impacts on practice is contained in the recent publication, *A Good
Practice Guide: Health and safety of pupils on educational visits* (DfEE 1998). This
book recognizes that most school visits take place without incident and that
teachers are already demonstrating a high level of safety awareness. However,
following the examination of a number of tragic incidents involving school children during recent years, a number of principles have been identified which
teachers are expected to use when making judgements.

Expert Witness Reports and the application of Case Law are another source
of useful information. In the past ten years there has been a gradual increase in
case-study material available for analysis. Informal analysis suggests that
teachers have been confronted by a number of cases which question their 'duty
of care', with more and more cases alleging negligence based on injury. The
emerging issues raise concern about the level of supervision, teaching methods,
transportation and, more recently, individual rights (gender, special needs, etc.).

One 'high profile' case was that involving the role of the official in sporting
contests. The Smoldon v. Whitworth (1996) court case received extensive
publicity and the outcome is of great significance not only for referees of rugby
matches but for all those involved in any other refereed contest. Smoldon
succeeded in a claim for negligence against the referee of a game of colts rugby
in which he suffered a broken neck. Whilst this was not directly related to
primary school physical education Judge Curtis's decision has resulted in many
school authorities and adults involved in the running of school sports to recon-
sider their duty of care. The decision is described as particularly noteworthy as it
breaks new ground, not previously contemplated, in allocating responsibility for
sports injuries suffered by children and young persons (Monitor Press 1999).
The case exposed the referee as the person who is placed in control of the game
and therefore the key person who is able to prevent any foreseeable harm to
players. Justice Curtis noted there was a general foreseeable risk of serious injury
to certain players in the game of rugby and in his view it was just and reasonable
for the law of negligence to seek to protect players from 'unnecessary and potentially highly dangerous, if not lethal aspects of the game by the imposition of a

duty of care'. The final ruling considered that the referee had fallen below the standard expected of a reasonably competent referee. This decision did hold that the referee should bear some or all of the loss that junior rugby players suffer if they do not show 'reasonable competence' in controlling the game so as to safeguard the players from foreseeable risks or foreseeable injury.

The outcome did have implications for future understandings of the role and responsibilities of the referee, be they in charge of a school or club game. What is clear is that a teacher refereeing a school game would be expected to assume much more responsibility for the welfare of pupils in a school match than players in a match at senior level. This is due to the different level of skill and maturity of the players involved. Mr Justice Curtis did suggest that in school matches the referee's role might extend beyond controlling the game and include a duty to instruct the players so that they might participate without fear of injury. Furthermore, the referee's responsibility includes the conditions under which the game is to be played. This relates to the condition of a facility and any potential hazards.

Whilst this is a relatively new area in British case law, tort litigation against contest officials has increased in America. Not surprisingly many of the issues discussed by Justice Curtis have long been on the American agenda. Koehler summarized the emerging areas of potential liability as

> Negligence in the supervision or control of the contest.
> Failure to stop an athletic contest when a player appeared to be in danger of serious injury.
> Not prohibiting a contest from being played.
> Failure to stop an athletic contest, once begun, due to the physical conditions of the playing surface.
>
> (Koehler 1991: 14)

Finally, there is no reason to believe that the principle underpinning the Smoldon v. Whitworth decision is limited to rugby. The principle applies to other games such as cricket, rounders and hockey where unskilled players may pose a risk to the welfare of other players. Whether it is a referee or umpire or other adult in charge of the game, Mr Justice Curtis did state that 'no responsible player and no responsible referee had anything to fear' from this ruling, suggesting that teachers who fulfilled their professional responsibility and provided a duty of care have nothing to fear.

In order to develop a deeper understanding of teachers' views about safety and the circumstances in which they work the National Unit for Safety across the Curriculum (NUSAC) commissioned a research study into teachers' practice, anxieties and personal concerns about safety (Raymond and Thomas 1998). Over 200 primary schools in the south-west of England were initially sent a questionnaire and a small sample of 10 schools was involved in a follow-up interview. The evidence clearly suggests that the majority of teachers declared themselves less than familiar with their formal responsibilities under health and safety law. Furthermore, this impacted on the curriculum they made available to pupils, with many teachers adopting a 'negligence avoidance' strategy rather that taking any chances. Few teachers reported access to ongoing further professional development to help them cope with their concerns. Teachers expressed feelings of insecurity and worry and these were not surprising given the limited amount of physical education many class teachers experience in their initial teacher training. This lack of time was confirmed in a recent report on the preparation of non-specialist primary trainees on both undergraduate and postgraduate courses. A sample of 20 partnerships between schools and higher education institutions revealed a number of significant weaknesses in the quality of trainees' professional skills (Ofsted 1998).

What Does this all Mean for Physical Education in the Primary School?

There is no doubt that teachers are acutely aware of the need to create a safe learning environment for all pupils. However, if teachers are to improve their understanding of their responsibilities and how these interact with the law, increase their knowledge of safety and begin to feel more comfortable with managing risk then they need access to up-to-date relevant research findings and reports of other people's experiences. Being informed about how and why accidents happen can help us reflect on our own practice. The ultimate aim is to continue offering children a challenging curriculum in which they experience and manage risk so that they are extended and able to maximize their potential. Following an accident hindsight is a wonderful thing. What we have to do is to try and foresee any potential hazards and accidents.

Understanding the legal system is important – teachers need to know the implications of alleged negligence and how their practice will be scrutinized. Various authors with an interest in physical education and the legal system offer us much useful guidance. Lowe suggests that in deciding whether an accident was caused by negligence or not, a court will consider:

- the reasonableness of the conduct of the activity
- the numbers involved
- the layout of the area
- the instructions given to the pupils
- whether the conduct of the lesson was generally in accordance with normal practice in physical education teaching and the practices of the school
- the experience of the teacher
- the age and aptitude of the pupils involved.

(Lowe 1998: 40)

Similar guidance is offered by BAALPE, who also remind teachers that a charge of negligence is easier to refute if all reasonable steps have been taken to ensure the safety of the working environment and equipment (1995: 24). Negligence is the failure to do what a *reasonable* person would have done in the circumstances, or doing what a reasonable person would not have done in the circumstances. Reasonableness is the key word (Croner 1996: 3–51). Bramwell offers a further set of questions used to ascertain if the school was negligent:

- Could the accident have been prevented – in other words was the accident foreseeable?
- Was the activity undertaken and the equipment being used appropriate to the age and experience of the children?
- Were the children given adequate warnings about the danger of misusing equipment?
- Did the organisation of the lesson follow normal and accepted practice?
- Did the teacher involved follow/stick to school/LEA policy?
- Did the child receive swift and effective attention after the accident?

(Bramwell 1993: 32)

This type of guidance is useful for teachers to use as a framework for their own school policy and practice in safety management.

Concluding Comments

Whilst teachers can draw on research findings and relevant work in relation to good practice, these can only support not substitute for the teacher's decision-making responsibilities (Hellison and Templin 1991: 5). It must be remembered that teachers know best the capabilities of their pupils and the circumstances in which they are teaching. They must be allowed to exercise a certain amount of professional judgement. That said, this professional judgement must reflect regular and approved practice and so all teachers need to try to keep informed about research evidence and read more detailed publications, such as BAALPE *Safe Practice* (1995) and recent and relevant Health and Safety guidance. Teachers need to be aware that safety advice can, and does, change. They have a professional responsibility to keep up-to-date, by watching out for safety advice in professional journals, the *Bulletin* published by BAALPE, the *British Journal of Physical Education* and HSE publications, curriculum guidance from the Qualification and Curriculum Authority, DfEE and LEAs, as well as research-based papers in journals. However, in order for teachers to be able to undertake this they must negotiate regular access to opportunities for their continuing professional development.

Notes

1 Tragedies examined: Altwood School 1988 where four boys died on an educational

visit to the Austrian Alps; the case of Van Oppen v. Bedford Charity Trustees in 1989 where a pupil was seriously injured as he attempted to rugby tackle an opponent; the death of pupils whilst on a canoeing trip in Lyme Bay 1993.

Readers must be aware that the recommendations made in this chapter have no legal status and are only offered as guidance, which is available at the time of publication.

References

BAALPE (1995) *Safe Practice in Physical Education*. Dudley: Dudley LEA.

——(1998) *Achieving Excellence as a Subject Leader in Physical Education: Exemplification of the National Standards for Subject Leaders*. Dudley: Dudley LEA.

Bramwell, A. (1993) 'A cautionary tale of negligence', *Management in Education* 17, 1, 32–3.

Croner (1996) *Head's Legal Guide*. Kingston upon Thames: Croner Publications.

——(1998) 'Teaching safely and teaching safety', *School Health and Safety Briefing* 15, January.

DES (1992) *Physical Education in the National Curriculum*. London: HMSO.

DfE (1995)*Teachers Pay and Conditions Document*. London: HMSO.

DfEE (1998) *A Good Practice Guide: Health and safety of pupils on educational visits.*London: HMSO.

——(1998) *Teaching High Status, High Standards: Requirements for courses of initial teacher training*. Circular 10/98. London: HMSO.

Hellison, D. and Templin, T. (1991) *A Reflective Approach to Teaching Physical Education*. Champaign, IL: Human Kinetics.

HMSO (1974) *Health and Safety at Work Act*. London: HMSO.

——(1992) *Management of Health and Safety at Work*. London: HMSO.

——(1995) *The Reporting of Injuries, Disease and Dangerous Occurrences Regulations (RIDDOR)*. London: HMSO.

Koehler, R. W. (1991) *Law, Sport Activity and Risk Management*. Champaign, IL: Stripes Publishing Co.

Lowe, C. (1998) *The Clear Guide to Health, Safety and Security in Education*. Birmingham: Questions Publishing Co.

Metzler, M. (1990) *Instructional Supervision in Physical Education*. Champaign, IL: Merrill.

Monitor Press Ltd (1998) *A Review of Education Law: A special report*. Suffolk: Monitor Press Ltd.

Ofsted (1998) *Teaching Physical Education in the Primary School: The initial training of teachers*. London: Ofsted.

Raymond, C.W. and Thomas, S.M. (1998) 'Health and safety legislation: teachers' current practice and anxieties in physical education', unpublished manuscript. Exeter: NUSAC.

Siedentop, D (1989) 'The effective elementary specialist study', *Journal of Teaching in Physical Education* 8, 3, Monograph.

Silverman, S. (1991) 'Research on teaching in physical education, *Research Quarterly for Exercise and Sport* 62, 4, 352–64.

Teacher Training Agency (TTA)(1998) *National Standards for Subject Leaders*. London: Teacher Training Agency.

Thomas, S. M. (1994) 'Adventure education: risk and safety out of school', in S.M. Thomas (ed.) *Outdoor Education Perspectives* 50.

7 Girls' Experience of Physical Education

Voting With Their Feet?

Julie Bedward and Anne Williams

Introduction

Amid the current concern for underachievement among boys, beginning in the primary school, and emerging across the curriculum, physical education remains one subject where there is still evidence, particularly at secondary level, of girls' underachievement, relative lack of opportunity and negative attitudes. It appears that the opportunity provided by the introduction of the National Curriculum to address the traditionally gendered nature of physical education (Scraton 1992) was missed (Williams 1996, Williams and Woodhouse 1996, Williams and Bedward 1999). This is despite the recognition by the original physical education working group of the potential of the impending orders and guidance for changing practice (DES 1992). This chapter explores some implications of research carried out in the secondary context, for the primary school teacher.

A recent survey for Ofsted on research into gender differences makes virtually no reference to physical education (Arnot et al. 1998). An earlier publication based upon a survey of good practice in physical education (Ofsted 1995) makes relatively little reference to gender issues, although it does highlight the need to examine the issue of differential access to extra-curricular activities, with boys tending to have more provision than girls. Good practice in the primary school was not defined at any point in relation to equitable opportunities for boys and girls except in relation to extra-curricular opportunities. Here evidence about primary school participation rates was apparently unavailable, although reference is made to higher numbers of male than female participants at secondary level. Scrutiny of the Ofsted reports of 120 primary schools in six LEAs reveals no reference to gender issues in relation to physical education. Given some of the issues raised by Leaman (1984, 1988), Pollard (1988) and Clarricoates (1980) which suggested that there could be considerable difficulties facing the teacher in co-educational primary school classes, and that there were gender issues related to primary school children's access to playground space, this suggests that there has either been significant change, or that these issues were not addressed during the course of the inspection. The latter seems more likely, given the nature of the framework and the guidance provided for inspectors for physical education, although a separate section on equal opportunities does make reference to equality of access including girls' access to play spaces (Ofsted 1998).

The evidence discussed in this chapter is based on a study conducted between September 1997 and December 1998 that focused on the impact of recent policy on the provision of physical education and sporting opportunities for female adolescents. The study constituted an in-depth exploration of issues relating to gender differences in the provision of physical education in secondary schools. The context of the study was the introduction and subsequent revision of the National Curriculum for Physical Education, and the emergence during the mid-1990s of sport and physical education as political issues. It follows an earlier study (Williams and Woodhouse 1996) which analysed pupil attitudes towards National Curriculum physical education drawing on a sample of 3,000 students from eight secondary schools.

Our evidence is based on fieldwork carried out between October 1997 and March 1998 in three secondary schools: School A was multicultural and situated on the urban fringe in a working-class area; School B was an inner-city multicultural single-sex school with approximately 50 per cent of students on its roll being Muslims; and School C was a middle-class suburban school with a mainly white European intake. Data consisted of semi-structured interviews with pupils and teachers and observation of physical education lessons in all three schools. Ninety one pupils, 87 of whom were female, and 12 teachers were interviewed. Our sample consisted of students with a range of attitudes towards physical education: some enjoyed all aspects of the subject, others hated PE, and many came mid-way between these two extremes and enjoyed some aspects and activities more than others. Similarly, some were extremely able sportswomen, others struggled in most physical activities, and many had levels of ability ranging between these two extremes. A number of factors influenced students' attitudes to physical education. Of particular relevance to the primary school teacher are findings related to activities, self-concept, and uniform rules and we will concentrate on these areas.

Activities

Students had clear and well-developed activity preferences. Gymnastics and dance were either loved or hated by pupils. In gymnastics this was closely related to personal ability. In dance, enjoyment was often attributed to the opportunities offered for creativity and expression. Those who disliked gymnastics found it humiliating, a view often exacerbated by negative body concepts among those who perceived themselves as overweight. Dislike of dance was often attributed to boredom, to the teaching approach adopted or to the presence of boys. Athletics, like gymnastics and dance, attracted opposing views, with positive attitudes strongly related to ability. Many students found the experience of performing badly in front of their peers humiliating. Others disliked it because of its competitiveness. However, the variety of running, throwing and jumping events was popular because it offered students an element of choice, and a chance to perform at different types of activity.

The already well-documented dislike by many girls of winter team games, was confirmed again by our sample although, for many, team games were a source of considerable enjoyment and success. The relatively low levels of interest in competitive games and particularly competitive team games, among adolescent girls is well known (Williams 1988; Sports Council 1995). In the primary school context the issues are rather different. Adolescent girls' attitudes are affected by their perceptions of their ability, the conditions in which winter team games are frequently played and, all too often, the uniform which they are required to wear. Given that most primary school children have not reached the stage of distinguishing between effort and ability as determinants of success (Ewing 1981, Buchan and Roberts 1992), the effect of ability upon their atti- tudes to games is largely dependent upon the way games are taught (Roberts 1992). Provided that the teacher adopts strategies which promote inclusive prac- tice and which foster co-operation as well as competition, primary school pupils' attitudes remain positive. Much of the resentment felt by adolescents about conditions relate to playing hockey on cold days in muddy fields. This context is less evident in the primary school, where much games teaching takes place on a hard playing area, and where lack of adequate showering or washing facilities precludes taking children out to get covered in mud. Good primary school prac- tice also includes a wider range of games than those typically available at KS3 and more variety in the form of adapted and small sided games. Few primary schools have the rigid physical education uniform policies that remain in some secondary schools; however our evidence does underline the need to allow pupils to participate in clothing which keeps them warm and with which they feel comfortable.

A further issue which emerged was the students' own perceptions of sexism within the curriculum. That is, they considered the division of sports along traditional lines into boys' and girls' games was sexist. The retention of a gender-differentiated PE curriculum within secondary education is an anomaly that seems inappropriate to young people, who in the late 1990s have experi- enced most of their education within a framework of equal opportunities. Within all our research schools, most winter games were divided into either boys' or girls' activities. Most girls within our research schools were denied the opportunity to pursue football, rugby, cricket and basketball within PE lessons, whilst the only activity not available to boys was netball.

When students were asked to identify any activities in which they felt that only boys or girls should participate, virtually every student denounced that approach as sexist and expressed the view that both sexes should have the opportunity to pursue all activities. In particular most of the girls felt it was unfair that they were denied the opportunity to play football, which was the most popular out-of-school game amongst the girls in our earlier study

(Williams and Woodhouse 1996). Many of the girls had played football at primary school and thought it was unfair that this was not offered to them at secondary school. One student from the United States who began her British education in Year 9 found the concept of traditional male and female sports very strange:

> We played it almost every other day [football in US schools]. I've never played it at all since I came here. Not at all. When I came here, the first thing I asked was, 'What do you do in gym time?'. And they go, 'Well, the girls play these sports and the guys play those sports'. 'Well, why can't the girls play those sports also?'. And they go, 'Well, that's the way it was set up and we don't just change it just because one person can play it'. And I go, 'But why?'. It's really different that way. And it gives everyone a chance to kind of co-exist. I mean we're in the nineties now; we're going into the twenty-first century. We can't keep living in the past.
>
> (BL, Year 9 student)

Many of the girls identified football as their favourite winter team game, and considered it unfair that this activity was not available to them within PE lessons. Many enjoyed playing football with friends and family outside school, and expressed frustration that they were less skilled than the males they played with because, unlike girls' physical education, boys' PE tended to be centred around football. However, some of our interviewees were talented footballers and were involved with women's league football. Unusually, one of these students who was taking GCSE PE had selected football as her main sport. This had been permitted by the PE staff because she was a very able player. However, as the only girl taking football within the GCSE group, she was the only girl in an all-male group. By failing to offer football to girls within PE lessons, this reduces the options available to many of them if they pursue GCSE PE. Even students who did not express a desire to play football considered it was unfair that this sport was not offered to girls at school. Several girls also would have liked to have seen rugby offered as a winter team game. Several of these had played this game at primary school and enjoyed it.

Although many of our sample had played football at primary school and some had played rugby, these games had still not been as widely available to them as they had been to boys. Earlier research into primary school pupils' perceptions of gender issues related to sport and physical education (Williams 1989) suggests that children have well-developed, often gender specific, views by the end of KS1. More recent evidence (Arnot et al. 1998) suggests that views may be becoming less gendered, although boys' roles remain more rigidly prescribed than girls' (Henshaw et al. 1992). This suggests that primary school children today will be as able as our secondary school students to articulate a view about their physical education practice and will be well aware of the sexist nature of provision which offers activities to one gender but not to the other.

Whilst many of the PE teachers we spoke to recognized that football was popular with girls, they often did not consider it to be a suitable activity to offer to them in PE lessons. The reasons given for this included female teachers not feeling competent to teach football, and because football was a contact sport it was considered inappropriate to offer as a mixed-sex activity. This suggests that in-service training is needed for both primary and secondary school teachers to raise awareness of equal opportunity issues and to equip them with the knowledge and understanding needed to teach football.

Uniform

Quite often a student's general dislike of physical education was in part attributed to the PE kit that had to be worn. The uniform required for PE varied at each school with some of the PE departments demonstrating a greater degree of sensitivity towards female adolescents than others. Most of the students accepted the need for a PE kit but felt this should apply just to the colour of garments worn. The preferred clothing for most students was shorts, jogging bottoms, T-shirts and sweatshirts; this was equated to the type of clothing students would choose to wear for physical activities pursued outside school.

At school A the standard games kit was a T-shirt and games skirt. Jogging bottoms could be worn by Muslim students and by other students when the teacher decreed it was cold enough outside for trousers to be worn. Jumpers and sweatshirts could also be worn if the teacher decided it was cold enough. PE knickers had to be worn underneath the skirts. It was quite common to find many students playing netball during November and December in T-shirts and skirts. The policy of only allowing trousers to be worn by Muslim girls was considered to be very unfair both by the non-Muslim and Muslim students who perceived this policy as racist:

> I think sometimes if you just want to wear blue tracksuit bottoms I think you should, because you know the Asian people they wear tracksuit bottoms because they can't show their legs.
>
> (TU, Year 11 student)

> But some people want to wear jogging bottoms too, and they get told off for bringing them ... and they get into detention for not bringing the proper kit, because they're supposed to wear mini skirts and stuff like that. ... it's not fair on them. We get to wear them, it's not fair for them though, because they want to as well, but they are not allowed.
>
> (TI, Year 9 student)

Interviewees from this school frequently complained that being made to play outdoor winter games in inadequate clothing in adverse weather conditions made PE lessons an unpleasant experience:

It's just that when it's cold and like if you were at home you wouldn't go out in a short skirt and a T-shirt and a jumper, but for PE we have to. We sometimes can't wear our trousers, and then you just get really cold and you think, 'Well, I can't do the sport, I'm too cold', and that just stops it really. It just puts you off it totally.

(HT, Year 9 student)

The girls simply required a more sensible, humane uniform policy that would allow them to wear trousers and sweatshirts in cold weather. This uniform policy existed at School B. At this school, the same winter games kit applied to all students; they could choose to wear either PE skirts or jogging bottoms. The students here were generally more satisfied with the kit requirements. Their main complaint centred on having to wear PE knickers underneath their skirts:

The PE skirts are really short, but you have to deal with it because that's the school uniform for PE. And you're not allowed to wear cycling shorts either. I don't think it's fair. ... We have to wear PE pants. Even though it's not showing your other pants, it's still a bit revealing I think.

(DF, Year 11 student)

This aspect of uniform rule was in force at all of the research schools. Many students expressed a preference for wearing cycling shorts, and many actually wore these for PE lessons despite being reprimanded:

If say you're chubby and you want to wear shorts under your skirt because you get picked on, they (the teachers) don't understand. They always tell you to take them off, but you can't. Like today, we had to stand up whoever didn't have the right PE kit, and I got a warning. ... I thought it was embarrassing really because I wear shorts every PE lesson, and I get told off for that. I didn't do it. I didn't want to stand up, so I didn't do it.

(TE, Year 9 student)

At School C jogging bottoms could be worn by students for outdoor winter games. However, PE skirts had to be worn over the top of these. Many students felt this policy was impractical, 'the skirts get in the way', and others pointed out that the two garments worn together looked ridiculous. Whilst PE skirts were considered inadequate clothing for winter games, many students also felt uncomfortable wearing short skirts. Many students stated a preference for wearing shorts, or being allowed to wear cycling shorts underneath the skirts. At School C PE skirts also had to be worn for gymnastics and many of the girls felt embarrassed and restricted by this policy. At both Schools A and B, leggings and long T-shirts were worn for gymnastics and dance. Most felt comfortable with this and felt less self-conscious because they were allowed to wear loose fitting T-shirts over the leggings.

At school A the uniform policy was strictly enforced and students received detentions and had points deducted from their overall PE grades if incorrect uniform was worn. Several of the sample students felt so self-conscious wearing PE skirts they refused to wear them and stoically accepted the penalties incurred for wearing their preferred items of shorts or jogging bottoms:

> We're not supposed to play in our shorts, but I still do, because it doesn't really matter what we wear, it's whether we do it or not. ... Miss T, she usually has a go at us and everything. I'm sorry but I think it's just wrong all the marking and everything that they're doing. ... If we're wearing shorts, we get marks knocked off. By the end of the lesson, we don't really get any marks, but at least we've done it.
>
> (NO, Year 11 student)

> The teacher knocks us down in our monthly merit marks [for not wearing PE skirts]. ... Like if I wear my skirt then I won't enjoy it, so it's not worth it to get a high mark. I'd rather enjoy it.
>
> (NI, Year 11 student)

Students overwhelmingly expressed a preference for wearing practical clothing for PE which they felt comfortable in. For many of the girls, PE skirts did not meet this requirement. A simple measure of modifying uniform policy to include the wearing of jogging bottoms and shorts could overcome many of the problems identified by students.

These concerns are also of considerable relevance to the primary school teacher. While uniform policy for physical education in the primary school tends to be less rigid than that reported by some of our sample, issues about appropriate wear for cold weather conditions, about embarrassment caused by wearing of some garments in mixed gender lessons and equitable treatment for all pupils do apply. Certainly many girls at KS2 are acutely embarrassed at having to do physical education dressed in pants and T shirt or with a games skirt rather than shorts.

Ability/Self-Concept

Student ability within different activity areas certainly impacted on their enjoyment of these. While this is to some extent inevitable, feelings were exacerbated in many cases by a lack of sensitivity leading to organizational practices that expose students to pressure from more able peers or to unnecessary public humiliation. Several students complained that teachers focused only on the more able performers during lessons. This added to their frustration of lacking ability at a certain activity because they also felt it denied them the possibility of improvement. Students often attributed their dislike of various activities to their not being good at them. Several students described feeling excluded in team games where they felt play was dominated by the most able players:

It's just sometimes you get left out, and it keeps on going to the good players. And they get more attention if they're good at it.

(TI, Year 9 student)

NO: And if you're not very good, you don't get the ball.
BM: Yes, because nobody passes it to you.
NO: And you'll have someone who reckons they're God, and gets the ball and they'll just try and beat everyone.
BM: Take on the team all by themselves.

(NO and BM, Year 11 students)

Others particularly disliked dance and gymnastics if they were not talented at these because these activities involve performances in front of the class:

I did a bit of dance. It's all right, but I feel kind of stupid going round and round, you know. And a couple of times I have had to do it in front of the whole class and it's really embarrassing. So I don't think I like that either.

(BS, Year 11 student)

[Gymnastics is TE 's least favourite activity because of] Showing it in front of everybody, I suppose, and trying to jump on to those massive boxes that I can't do. It's really embarrassing.

(TE, Year 9 student)

Similarly, students who performed poorly in athletics events often disliked these activities because they experienced humiliation in front of their peers. The performance aspect of batting in rounders by students who found it difficult to hit the ball resulted in their dislike of this game:

And because people are watching you more so with rounders, because everyone is watching the person with the bat.

(NE, Year 11 student)

Negative judgements about their ability from either peers or teachers could also affect students' enjoyment of particular activities. Failure to be selected by teachers to play in school teams could lead to students rejecting that particular activity:

I found the teachers, like if you couldn't do it, they didn't seem to have much interest in you, and you were made to feel stupid.

(DY, Year 11 student)

> And they don't encourage you. They only encourage the people who are in the teams; everybody doesn't try then, because the teacher only coaches whoever's in the team.
>
> (MD, Year 11 student)

Several students referred to hurtful comments made by class members that contributed to their development of hatred for particular activities:

> I'm not very graceful really. I'm just not very good at it [gym], so I got laughed at a bit for doing it, which wasn't very good. ... They're probably just as good as me, but I'm a bit – well I wouldn't say I'm fat, but I'm bigger than the rest of them. They tend to shrug off their embarrassment of doing it by saying something about me instead. Not particularly maliciously, but it does tend to put you off a bit.
>
> (LC, Year 11 student)

With team games in particular, students who were able players, often those who played in school teams, expressed a dislike for playing these games in PE lessons as they found the pace of the game too slow and the focus on skill development tedious.

Adolescent girls are often very concerned about their physical appearance, and several students expressed concerns about their body shape and weight during interviews. For some girls, such concerns led them to view physical education and all forms of exercise positively as they considered that involvement in physical activity was a good way of controlling their weight. Other students who considered themselves overweight often experienced embarrassment during physical education lessons. Being overweight was often seen as contributing to poor performance in PE; in particular, dance and gymnastics were often experienced as an ordeal. These problems were often exacerbated by uniform policy, in particular having to wear short PE skirts, and showers were also often dreaded. Students who were small for their age also experienced problems in PE. Differences between students in terms of ability, shape and size can often be made explicit with in the context of PE lessons. To minimize the negative impact that these differences may have on a student's self concept, sensitive policies in relation to uniform, showering and organization of activities need to be pursued.

The attitude of peers and their behaviour could affect students' enjoyment of physical education. Our findings provide further evidence of what Laws and Fisher describe as 'numerous examples of personal embarrassment related to public displays during competition sometimes associated with letting other team members down and sometimes with having one's incompetence highlighted for all to see' (1999: 30). Team games, in particular were unpopular with less able players who complained of cruel comments and 'bitchiness' from other players on the team. Some students described how these criticisms could continue beyond the PE lesson and could be very unpleasant. These types of comments were often noticed by the researcher during lesson observation, in particular during team games. On none of these occasions did the teachers intervene and check criticisms. It would seem that competitiveness and the desire to win are often considered desirable. Criticism of players who are perceived as letting the team down is therefore considered justified. This results in less able players feeling excluded and vulnerable during team games. Playing in teams with less able students is often a source of frustration for able players who are enthusiastic about PE. Many of these girls were very critical of peers who lacked motivation, and who they claimed spoilt team games by not putting any effort into playing. These comments demonstrate that some of the arguments used against mixed-sex team games are equally applicable to mixed-ability team games. This evidence from the secondary school context is consistent with that reported, albeit some time ago, by Evans (1985) and Evans and Roberts (1987) with reference to younger pupils. They point to the exclusion of less able 8–12-year-olds from games, both when teams are picked and during play.

Our research would seem to suggest that within the context of the provision of National Curriculum physical education, girls are disadvantaged in relation to boys. The disadvantaged position of girls would seem to have little to do with the recent implementation of policy and more to do with the remarkable resilience to change that physical education has demonstrated, particularly over the last 15 years (Scraton 1992). The failure to abandon a traditional gender-differentiated approach has resulted in physical education being unique among subjects within British secondary education. The continuing failure to provide equal opportunities for boys and girls within physical education results in girls being offered less choice of activity than boys. The retention of a traditional gender-segregated provision was identified and criticized as sexist by virtually every student we interviewed. While opportunities at primary level may be more equal within the curriculum, extra-curricular provision is much more likely to be an issue, as there is considerable evidence to suggest that staffing provision for girls is much more problematic than for boys, even though primary school staff rooms are predominantly female. Few of our findings are new, but it is disappointing to find such gendered practice after more than 20 years work towards more equitable educational provision for girls and boys. It would seem that the introduction of National Curriculum physical education constituted a missed opportunity to revise out-dated practices of gender-differentiated physical education. Although these findings relate specifically to adolescent girls, many of them are equally applicable to younger children.

Implications

We suggest that there are several important messages here for the primary school teacher. First, the retention of a broad programme of activities, particularly at KS2 is an important factor in ensuring that pupils leave primary school with positive physical education experiences which can form the basis of continued success at KS3. Second, primary schools should make every attempt to ensure that girls continue to have access to the same range of activities as boys. The issue in relation to access to football, raised by almost every girl interviewed in our study, has implications for the primary school, not only within curriculum provision, but, more significantly, with reference to extra-curricular opportunities. Third, the potential negative impact of inappropriate expectations with respect to uniform should be recognized. Primary schools rarely have uniform for physical education in the way that most secondary schools have explicit expectations. Nevertheless, at a time when many girls reach puberty before they leave the primary school, the appropriateness of wearing T shirt and knickers in mixed gender lessons, or of wearing short skirts, has to be questioned. Fourth, the importance of identifying and implementing organizational and teaching strategies that enhance rather than diminish self-esteem should be noted. Research discussed elsewhere (see Chapter 1) suggests that it is not until the end of KS2 that most children begin to distinguish between effort and ability as determinants of success. The same research taken together with our evidence, suggests that the teacher plays a major role in either promoting a positive self-image, or in inflicting damage through exposing children, particularly those coping with the physical changes of puberty, to experiences which they may find humiliating. Given sensitive and informed teaching, there is no reason why children of all abilities should not find primary school physical education a positive and enjoyable learning experience. This would be consistent with the intention expressed in the National Curriculum consultation (QCA 1999), that physical education provision should be inclusive and enable all pupils to learn effectively and safely.

Acknowledgements

The writers would like to acknowledge the support of the Nuffield Foundation, which supported the research reported in this chapter (Project reference HQ/290).

References

Arnot M., Gray J., James, M. and Rudduck, J. (1998) *Recent Research on Gender and Educational Performance*. London: The Stationery Office.

Buchan, F. and Roberts, G.C. (1991) 'Perceptions of success of children in sport', unpublished manuscript, University of Illinois. Cited in M. Lee (ed.) *Coaching Children in Sport*, London: E&F Spon.

Clarricoates, K. (1980) 'The importance of being Ernest ... Tom ... Jane: the perception and characterisation of gender conformity and gender deviation in primary schools', in R. Deem (ed.) *Schooling for Women's Work*. London: Routledge & Kegan Paul.

DES (1991) *Physical Education for Ages 5–16: Proposals of the Secretary of State for Education and Science and the Secretary of State for Wales*. London: DES.

Evans, J. (1985) 'The process of team selection in children's self-directed and adult-directed games', PhD dissertation. University of Illinois.

Evans, J. and Roberts, G.C. (1987) 'Physical competence and the development of children's peer relations, *Quest* 39, 23–35.

Ewing, M.E. (1981) 'Achievement orientation and sports behavior in males and females'. PhD thesis, University of Illinois. Cited in M. Lee (ed.) *Coaching Children in Sport*. London: E & F Spoon.

Henshaw, A., Kelly, J. and Gratton, C. (1992) 'Skipping for girls: children's perceptions of gender roles and gender preferences, *Educational research* 34, 2, 229–35.

Laws, C. and Fisher, R. (1999) 'Pupils' interpretations of physical education', in C.A. Hardy and M. Mawer (eds) *Learning and Teaching in Physical Education*. London: Falmer Press.

Leaman, O. (1984) *Sit on the Sidelines and Watch the Boys Play: Sex differentiation in physical education*. London: Longman.

——(1988) 'Competition, co-operation and control', in J. Evans (ed.) *Teachers, Teaching and Control in Physical Education*. Brighton: Falmer Press.

Ofsted (1995) *Physical Education: A survey of good practice*. London: HMSO.

——(1998) *Inspecting Subjects 3–11: Guidance for inspectors*. London, Ofsted.

Pollard, A. (1988) 'Physical education, competition and control in primary education', in J. Evans (ed.) *Teachers, Teaching and Control in Physical Education*. Brighton: Falmer Press.

Roberts, G.C. (ed.) (1992) *Motivation in Sport and Exercise*. Champaign, IL: Human Kinetics.

QCA (1999) *The Review of the National Curriculum in England: The consultation materials*. London: QCA.

Scraton, S. (1992) *Shaping up to Womanhood: Gender and girls' physical education*. Buckingham: Open University Press.

Sports Council (1995) *Young People and Sport 1994*. London: Sports Council.

Williams, E.A. (1988) 'Physical activity patterns among adolescents: some curriculum implications, *Physical Education Review* 11, 28–39.

Williams, A. (1989) 'Girls and Boys Come Out to Play (but mainly boys): gender and physical education', in A. Williams (ed.) *Issues in Physical Education for the Primary Years*, Brighton: Falmer.

Williams, E.A. (1996) 'Problematising physical education practice: pupil experience as a focus for reflection', *European Journal of Physical Education* 1, 1, 19–35.

Williams, A. and Woodhouse, J. (1996) 'Delivering the discourse – urban adolescents' perceptions of physical education, *Sport, Education and Society* 1,2.

Williams, E.A. and Bedward, J. (1999) *Games for the Girls: The impact of recent policy on the provision of physical education and sporting opportunities for female adolescents*. Report to the Nuffield Foundation.

Towards Inclusion in Education and Physical Education

Tansin Benn

This chapter explores some of the issues and difficulties faced by teachers, students and pupils with particular reference to the interface of Islam and PE in primary schools. Discussion draws upon the findings of a four-year research project which revealed that it is not always easy 'being Muslim' in the English state education system, whether as a young child, an adolescent, a student teacher or qualified teacher (Benn 1998). Issues of understanding, valuing, respecting and including cultural diversity have rarely been so prominent. Central Europe is currently testimony to the atrocities of 'ethnic cleansing'. In 1997 the Runnymede Trust produced a damning report, 'Islamophobia – a challenge to us all', highlighting the depth and breadth of discrimination and prejudice suffered by British Muslims. The Stephen Lawrence inquiry (MacPherson 1999) recognized and probed issues of institutional racism in deep and public ways. A recent Ofsted report (1999) indicated failure within some parts of the education system to raise attainment of minority ethnic pupils or to effectively tackle racial tension and harassment in schools. Sharing research into the lived experiences of individuals from minority groups, as is attempted here, can help to increase understanding and to inform policy and practice.

The qualitative four-year research project involved tracking the life experiences of a volunteer group of seventeen self-declared Muslim women in initial teacher training (ITT), and seven of these in their early teaching careers in the primary sector. Methods were qualitative and included the collection of diary, interview and observation data. The majority of participants were British-born Muslims, of Asian, African-Asian and African-Caribbean heritage. The research focused on aspects such as: recollections from their own school days, day-to-day college-based experiences, professional development in their training and early careers, and other factors influencing daily experiences such as relationships with peers, tutors, class teachers, mentors, and family.

The opportunity to undertake the research came about as a result of the college targeting an increased number of ethnic minority students through offering an Islamic studies option on the B.Ed. programme. I was made head of the college's Physical Education Department at the time when a group of Muslim women students were approaching senior management to ask if changes could be made in PE to accommodate their religious requirements. What followed was a genuine attempt to increase understanding, and negotiate a way through any potential areas of conflict. The detail of this process of negotiated change is described elsewhere (Benn 1996). It is recognized that the experiences shared in this research belong in a particular time and place, but much was learned that offers potential for positive change towards more inclusive practice in and beyond PE.

Why Do Tensions Exist at the Interface of Physical Education and Islam?

Both are cultures, using 'culture' in its widest sense to embrace religion as an institution, like education, through which meanings, belief systems, values and patterns of life, are passed on as part of a group's heritage (Figueroa 1993: 91). The cultures of Islam and PE both encourage positive attitudes towards a fit and healthy body and to the positive benefits of exercise for girls and boys, women and men (Daiman 1995). This essential premise is not in dispute. Neither is the fact that such rhetoric is not reflected in reality, particularly in the lives of Muslim women, in many parts of the world, or in the lives of some Asian, Muslim girls in this country (Sfeir 1985; Carrington and Williams 1988; Kandiyoti 1992; Hargreaves 1994; Carroll and Hollinshead 1993).

One root of potential conflict between PE and Islam lies within the 'rituals' or 'traditions' of both cultures. The 'visibility' of PE and Islam, each with distinctive sets of principles, for example dress codes, different meanings attached to public and private use of the body, and particular gender role expectations, are areas for potential conflict (Hargreaves 1986; Mawdudi 1989). For example, in Islam, after puberty youngsters are required to dress modestly: boys are required to cover the body from navel to knee and girls to cover the body, arms and legs. Public nudity is forbidden, even in same-sex situations, as is free mixing of the sexes. For those who choose to adopt a more Islamic way of life girls may adopt the hijab, and Muslim pupils may more rigorously undertake religious practices, such as fasting during Ramadan and prayer rituals.

In PE particular dress codes and practices have developed over the last century. Curriculum and rituals are slow to change. Most primary pupils still change in mixed-sex classroom environments. Practices such as compulsory showering are becoming more 'optional' in places. Secondary PE experiences can be mixed-sex or single-sex, depending on feasibility and policy. 'Public PE spaces' such as netball courts, playing fields, central halls for indoor PE, or swimming pools with windows, are not conducive to preferences for privacy. As puberty for some children begins in the primary school and some families prefer a more Islamic upbringing for their young children, these issues could be raised in primary PE.

Where such traditions and rituals pull in opposite directions there may be difficulties. For example, where the Islamic requirement for modesty in dress code counters the PE/sports requirements to wear, often in the name of safety, dress that is relatively revealing of the body such as leotards, swimming trunks and games skirts or shorts. So struggles can emerge over how the body looks and behaves. Anxiety underpins the tensions under discussion. For some Muslims for whom maintenance of the Islamic way of life is central to their identity there is anxiety about religious transgression. In PE there is anxiety about 'lowering standards' in traditional curriculum practice amongst the 'gatekeepers' of the profession: 'particular people setting standards, making decisions ... [acting] to protect what is seen to be right and correct' (Talbot 1990: 116). In both PE and Islam, cultural practices are 'embodied': meanings are encoded and maintained in practices involving the body. For those with deep commitment to either arena, accommodation is likely to be problematic since change can bring a sense of loss or gain to individuals affected (Sparkes 1990).

The research project took me on a journey with the Muslim women through their recollections of PE during their own primary and secondary school experiences, through their initial teacher training (ITT) curriculum PE courses and their early career experiences of teaching the subject. Within the broader picture, evidence indicated that those women who wore the hijab (headscarf/Islamic dress) as an outward (public) and inward (private) symbol of Islamic faith, had the 'hardest time' in schools, training and teaching. They were sometimes victims of religious prejudice and discrimination, evident in the words, silences or actions of others: teachers, lecturers, advisers, head teachers, colleagues, parents and children. Unless they were employed in a former 'school experience' school, jobs were difficult to secure and hostility towards their Muslim identity was common. This is not to suggest that all Muslim women are homogeneous, or experience the world in the same way, or 'suffer' in the state system. Neither is it to suggest that every non-Muslim is islamophobic. (Runnymede Trust 1997). It does highlight the need to contextualize the 'micro' research picture, and our understanding of the experiences of Muslims in PE, within a broader 'macro' social framework.

The Wider Social Context – Islamophobia in Britain

One of the reasons why it is not easy to be a 'visible' Muslim woman in many contexts in Britain is because islamophobia, 'the categorisation of Islam as homogenous, separatist and the natural enemy of the West' (Samad 1998), is a serious and dangerous feature of contemporary society. Incidents of exclusion, violence, prejudice and discrimination alongside stereotypical views of Muslims and in particular of the lives of Muslim women, provide the evidence (Runnymede Trust 1997). Largely fuelled by media attention to particular incidents, fear of Islam, assumptions about all Muslims and fundamentalism, and concerns about perceived abuses of Muslim women, are perpetuated. For example, a cartoon which appeared in the *Mail on Sunday* (10 August 1997: 51) encodes all three perspectives, ridiculing the practice of 'veiling' through a quip about the relationship of 'Diana and Dodi' just before the fatal Paris car crash in August 1997. In this wider context it is easier to understand why islamophobia is a 'challenge to us all'. As educators, we share responsibility to redress the balance by understanding more about Islam and by critically examining ways in which we include or exclude Muslim children and adults from participating in our culturally diverse, if unequal, society.

Tensions within and beyond Islam and PE

Gaining an objective view of historical or contemporary Islam is difficult. Despite a unified vision of faith, there is diversity in precise interpretation of Islamic religious texts and cultural perspectives which leads to continued conflicts within and between Muslim groups, as well as between Islamic and non-Islamic groups. Current increases in efforts for objective scholarly approaches to studying Islam will help, particularly the cause of Muslim girls and women:

> [Muslim] women have in many cases been deprived even of the most basic human rights advocated by Islam itself. Forced marriages, arbitrary divorces, female mutilations and other abuses are sadly common in the Muslim world, as are restrictions on women's education and on their role in the labour force ... we need to address these and other issues ... it is a question of appraising the reality of their suffering in the light of the authentic principles of justice and fairness, revealed in the Quran and practised in the early days of Islam by the Prophet and his Companions.
>
> (Jawad 1998, 5)

For the Muslim women in my research it was the possibility of studying Islam alongside their teacher training that helped to change their views of many things, including PE, in a positive direction. However, this did bring about other tensions, for example, when they started to challenge what they called 'Pakistani' and 'Bangladeshi' culture with their families:

> [we] are questioning and we look it up for ourselves, we say show us evidence, and we find a lot of things are not from Islam ... people are trying to find the real Islam again ... like women not being allowed to do PE, for no reason, just not allowed ... with the right facilities etc. we can ...
>
> (Zauda)

In relation to participation in PE, literature on the Islamic position is limited. Contributions by Carroll and Hollinshead 1993, Daiman 1995 and McGuire 1998 are welcome, although research into the area is problematic (see critique of Carroll and Hollinshead's work by Siraj-Blatchford 1993). There is more literature in relation to sport. The Islamic position on participation in sporting activity is positive. Participation in physical activities is encouraged in Islam for boys/men and girls/women. Examples from records of the life of the Prophet Mohammed are used to support the positive messages about sport and exercise, including encouragement for His wife and children, both boys and girls, to take part (Sfeir 1985; Daiman 1995). 'Islam exhorts its followers to take up sports and to inculcate this practice in their children at an early age. ... For nothing in religion or tradition bars this' Naciri (1973, 600).

Globally the evidence of Muslim participation in physical activities is uneven but suggests there are particular problems for Muslim women in the area of competitive sport (Kamiyole 1986; Zouabi 1975; Sfeir 1985; Hargreaves 1994). Ahmed (1992) suggests this is rooted in the contrast between 'ideological Islam' and 'establishment Islam': between the undoubted messages of equality in the Quran, for example in relation to legal rights, education and family role, and the political/legal Islam in which woman's position was 'fixed as subordinate'. Globally, unevenness of opportunity is evident in PE, where perceptions of the nature of the subject are often at the core of the problem. For example, amongst some African Muslim societies the perception of PE is one of 'play' rather than 'education'. Since 'play' is regarded as a distraction from higher order pursuits, the physical educator has even been regarded as an 'agent of Satan' (Kamiyole 1993, 20).

In Britain, tensions have been created by cultural practices which are regarded by some to be Islamic but which are not rooted in what others view as 'authentic or real Islam', such as not supporting women's participation in sport. Although evidence is scant, research in the Asian community is helpful since 95 per cent of British Muslims are of Asian origin. Figueroa (1993) makes an important point when he states that in some Asian communities sport and PE do not have the same cultural significance as in the dominant culture. There is evidence that some Asian parents do exercise greater control over their daughters' participation in community sport and some parents even withdraw them from PE (Carrington and Williams 1988). For these reasons, and the respect for *education* that does exist in these communities, keeping PE within a *compulsory* curriculum is essential since: 'physical education and school-sport activities ... are often the only type of sport parents allow their daughters to take part in' (De Knop et al. 1996). This is contradicted by McGuire and Collins (1998). Nevertheless, simplistic pathological explanations that place the 'problem' inside the Asian family have only delayed critical analysis of the sports/PE arenas.

Although the experiences of British Muslims in PE remain under-researched there are guidelines offered through the Muslim Educational Trust based in London which suggest that participation in PE is acceptable provided Islamic religious requirements are met (Sarwar 1994). Tensions related to the Muslim experience and PE in Britain emerge when religious requirements are not met. In such circumstances Sarwar's recommendation is to withdraw from PE, which results in a potentially serious conflict between state and religious requirements. In relation to other research that might be used to inform policy and practice,

Carroll and Hollinshead (1993) identified a number of problems for secondary-school age Muslim girls in relation to PE. These included dress, showers, Ramadan and timing of extra-curricular activities. However, this research was criticized by Siraj-Blatchford (1993) for ignoring institutional racism and issues of cross-structural research. According to Parker-Jenkins (1995) and Haw (1998), the situation for Muslim pupils is improving in schools. The 'PE experiences' encountered in my research, in one of England's most culturally diverse cities, indicate that there is still need for dialogue, understanding and negotiation, and that the needs of Muslim pupils *are* pertinent in primary schools.

Islam and Primary Physical Education

From the outset it is important to realize that education is not neutral but, rather, inevitably and unavoidably, privileges some interests and individuals over and above others:

> PE like all subject areas in the school curriculum is inevitably a site of struggle, a contest of and for competing definitions about what is to count as worthwhile knowledge, what the body, the individual, school and society are and ought to be.
>
> (Evans 1988, 2)

Physical Education has been part of the curriculum in this country for over a century. This period can be analysed as one of competing interest groups struggling to legitimize preferred ways of seeing the world. For example, gender tensions have permeated decision-making throughout that period and, more recently, political intervention and the increasing power-base of the sports lobby has influenced practice in PE. Nevertheless:

> For all the talk of reform in physical education in England and Wales and elsewhere, we can reflect that, in important respects very little has changed in the curriculum and pedagogies of physical education. Notable inequities have been sustained not only in 'official' documents, but also in their implementation.
>
> (Penney and Evans 1999, 138)

While cultural diversity has become increasingly a part of the make-up of contemporary British society, there is little evidence that cultural diversity 'has a strong voice' or is in any way influential, for example, in the making or re-making of the National Curriculum for PE. It is estimated that by 2001 one in three 16-year-olds, in the city in which this research was carried out, will be from black and ethnic minority groups. Currently only 5 per cent of the city's teachers are from these groups. Recruitment and retention of black and ethnic minority teachers is problematic. Perhaps greater acceptance of difference and diversity in the process of education would be less alienating. Evans et al. (1996, 3) describe the homogenizing educational experience attempted by the National Curriculum as setting out to make pupils 'more the same'. Such perceptions are exacerbated by the post-Dearing PE curriculum, which states that the dance curriculum should include ' some traditional dances of the British Isles' (DfE 1995), a statement which relies heavily on imaginative interpretation to warrant justification in contemporary Britain.

The primary PE curriculum is currently activity-focused, with gymnastics, games and dance being 'core' PE subjects for primary pupils and swimming being essential to the experiences of pupils between the ages of 5 and 11 years. Occasionally tensions do arise in relation to primary PE and the experiences of Muslim pupils. How do, and indeed should, teachers approach these issues? What knowledge and support do they draw upon and need to resolve tensions and meet the needs of both the statutory requirements for PE and the religious requirements of the local Muslim community? In initial teacher training, time for the study of equity issues has been eroded. Increasing centralized control of primary teachers' time, for example recent literacy and numeracy plans, have guaranteed less attention to subjects lower on the political agenda. Parallel moves to centralize teachers' activities, including schemes of work, further reduce flexibility for teachers to address diversity and difference in relation to their particular school context. Consciousness-raising can be achieved in other ways, such as through sharing aspects of my research project that illustrate the PE/Islam perspectives of a number of differently positioned people. These will include: the PE Adviser, Muslim pupils, Muslim student teachers, Muslim qualified teachers and Higher Education PE tutors.

The Adviser's Perspective: PE and Islam in the City

To contextualize the research into the interface of Islam and PE an in-depth interview was held with a local PE Adviser who had worked in the city for over 25 years. Tensions between different Muslim communities and primary PE had tended to 'come and go', to 'flare up and die down', but were usually resolved locally. Sometimes they 'flared up' when a new Imam joined a community, often from outside Britain, with different views. Specific issues of concern for Muslim communities were: dress, the mixed-sex nature of primary swimming, the public mixed-sex classroom changing experience in the primary school and occasionally dance. It was decided not to make central city policy on such issues since the needs of each community were different. As the Adviser reported:

> we started to look at city policy ... what we've found is [it is better] for each school to have their own independent policy – advised by us. We no longer say 'In the city all Muslim children will do this or that'.

Hard and fast rules ... put you in the middle and people use it against you ... it can stir up things that don't need to be stirred up.

A very small number of primary schools had taken the decision to provide single-sex swimming provision at primary level. The Adviser suggested that issues surrounding dance were perhaps the least 'resolvable'. This comment came after a difficult incident: 'we had an awful problem two years ago ... I think it comes from misunderstanding ... dance as an art form – they [some Muslim leaders] appear not to understand it.' Guidance to British Muslims from the Muslim Educational Trust is not supportive of this activity, creating a potential clash of state versus religious directive: 'Although it is one of the activities listed under PE (in the National Curriculum) it is our view that dance has no academic significance or value nor does it contribute positively to meaningful human knowledge' (Sarwar 1994, 13).

Part of the difficulty lies in the fact that, as with music, there is no consensus in Islam about these activities, and different views are held and practised between different Muslim sects (Parker-Jenkins 1995). However, dance in education was inevitably one activity area encountered by the Muslim women during their initial teacher training and early teaching careers. Their views on dance in education changed in the process of experiencing the college-based course. They were much more positive as a result of understanding rationale, principles and practice more fully. They were critical of damning statements made by those who may never have experienced or understood the nature of dance in the education context.

For the Adviser some negotiations had been difficult, exacerbated by the need to work through interpreters. He had encountered situations in which parents wanted to exclude their Muslim children on religious grounds. His 'bottom-line' was that any child who went to school in this country had an entitlement to the National Curriculum. PE was a statutory requirement and exclusion was only permissible through disapplication, which was not possible on religious grounds. Many complex issues underpin such negotiations but greater reciprocal knowledge and awareness, of Islamic requirements and of the clear intentions of PE and dance in education, would be invaluable to the negotiating process.

Muslim Pupils' Perspectives of PE

All the women in this research had been educated in British primary and secondary schools so PE had always been part of their experience. When asked to recollect those memories, accounts were mixed, both positive and negative. Significantly, the issues that remained most vivid were not related to the strong 'activities' focus in PE, for example experiences in gymnastics or games or dance. Memories were related to kit, mixed-sex environments, showers, particular teachers and their own family responses to their involvement in physical activities, including extra-curricular activities.

Infant PE memories held deep-rooted anguish for Zauda when she recalled having to 'tuck her vest into her pants'. She usually ended up crying until the teacher let her wear her vest loosely over her pants. Even at that age, and despite her mother's positive assurance that it was not a problem, she felt 'guilty' about revealing so much of her body in a mixed class. Secondary school memories also centred around 'coping strategies' or ways in which the Muslim women recollected surviving conflicts related to religious or cultural beliefs, for example when required to wear short games skirts they would 'pull skirts down and socks up to cover our legs'. Embarrassment about public changing sent some 'rushing to the toilets' and showering ensured some 'avoided PE', 'forgot towels' or had a 'series of colds'.

The degree to which the girls perceived themselves to be 'practising Muslims' (religiosity), whilst at secondary schools, affected their experiences in PE. For some the concept of 'religious transgression' did not arise until later in their lives when they were making a more conscious effort to move in an Islamic direction. This led to 'retrospective guilt' that they had participated in such kit and contexts whilst at secondary school. The majority of those who had been to all-girls secondary schools had more positive experiences than other pupils in mixed-sex environments. It could not be said that those Muslim girls attending predominantly Asian/Muslim state schools met any greater understanding than those in other types of schools did. The cultural context of the school – all-white, mixed, or majority Asian – was not the deciding factor in relation to positive or negative PE experiences.

Open or closed teachers' attitudes towards Asian and/or Muslim children, and towards accommodation of Islamic religious requirements, were the factors affecting the quality of the PE experiences recalled by the participants. Where there was understanding of religious requirements and acceptance of wearing track suits, privacy in changing and leniency in relation to the practice of showering, the Muslim girls had participated enthusiastically in PE and recalled happy experiences:

> I was the only Muslim in my school, and I was allowed to do whatever I needed to do. I could adapt the uniform. They said they would rather me do PE with jogging bottoms than not do PE at all so they used to allow that.
>
> (recorded in group interview)

Where rigid regimes were in place, stereotypical views of Asians or Muslims made clear, and little understanding or willingness to accommodate religious requirements offered, strong 'anti-PE' attitudes developed:

> As Muslim girls we weren't very encouraged in sports ... so many Asian girls are not good at sports.
>
> (Diary)

I sometimes get the impression that they seem to think us Asians are good for nothing when it comes to games. That's the attitude I also experienced at secondary school.

(recorded in diary)

Their parents were supportive of school-based PE with the 'educational' context ensuring a degree of approval to activities that were not considered a valued priority for Muslim females outside school. This finding supports De Knopp et al. (1996). After-school activities spilled over into time some preferred to direct elsewhere, although several of the Muslim women remembered representing their schools in a range of sports. Gazala recalled feeling disadvantaged because her parents did not understand that some all-female sporting opportunities were available and did meet Islamic requirements. Others felt resentment that their brothers were given greater freedom in the use of their spare time. All remained respectful to their parents and recognized changes in a more liberal direction as younger sisters were 'having an easier time than older sisters'. As their knowledge of Islam grew new tensions emerged for them as they began to challenge some community practices as 'Pakistani or Bangladeshi culture' and not what they described as 'real Islam' which referred to knowledge they were gaining through their Islamic studies.

Muslim Student Teachers' Perspectives of PE on School Experience

In relation to other school-based experiences the Muslim women had much in common with any student teachers during initial teacher training. Surviving school-based experience was challenging enough, for example with diverse cross-subject demands, duties, sorting roles and responsibilities, management of procedures, discipline, organization, and meeting other school expectations alongside college expectations for planning, assessment and evaluating. The Muslim women who had adopted the hijab, often also had to confront prejudices about their religious identity which came from senior managers, colleagues, pupils, and parents. Those most seriously affected by such difficulties often found themselves defending their right to be Muslim, responding to notions rooted in the stereotypical view that all Muslims are fundamentalists. This disadvantaged some in their efforts to become practising teachers.

In common with other students, lack of continuity and breadth of teaching PE on school experience emerged as a major concern. Lessons were cancelled or altered for various reasons at short notice, such as transport problems or alternative use of the hall. Despite strict instructions about the need for supervised teaching of PE, students sometimes found themselves without support, 'she [class teacher] said she had a lot to do'. Some articulated that they had been without good role models in relation to changing into PE kit, evidence of progression and continuity in planning and teaching, or evidence of any record-keeping in PE.

127

In relation to being Muslim, the PE experience was often 'better than anticipated'. This was sometimes related more to the low status of the subject in primary schools than the removal of anxieties about transgressing religious requirements. When in school, the issue of the presence of adult males in their PE lessons did not turn out to be as problematic as anticipated. Some had requested female tutors. Where male class teachers had been allocated, experiences turned out to be 'better than expected', especially in the case of PE 'specialist' tutors or class teachers who were able to offer subject support where confidence was low. Having an adult male present in a dance lesson would have been problematic for some of the research participants in that 'we could not teach in the way we would prefer – by getting involved'. Some were proactive to ensure this did not happen: 'I just asked my tutor not to come in to that session' which raises other issues for students in training such as safety, legal responsibilities and support to improve practice.

In their new roles as student teachers on school experience the Muslim women found themselves empathizing with tensions faced by Muslim pupils in PE yet feeling powerless to intervene. The three examples that follow offer illustrations of how lack of understanding of cultural difference and inflexible policy decisions on kit can alienate children as early as their infant years. In group interviews the Muslim women exchanged a number of incidents related to inflexible kit policies in their primary schools. They were aware that according to religious practice it was not until puberty that covering the legs and arms became 'officially' necessary but, equally, they were empathetic to the cultural practices parents wished to encourage during these primary years.

> All parents want to bring up their children in a way that will help the child to be a member of a community to 'fit in'. Here I am speaking more culturally than religiously. It would seen strange to bring a child up in a way that bears no resemblance to what you want that child to be when he grows up.
>
> (recorded in group interview)

Jamilah encountered a Muslim boy (6 years old) crying and refusing to get changed for PE. The teacher had little time for him in her anxiety to supervise the rest of a large infant class in changing and moving outside for PE. Jamilah was told this was a regular occurrence and that he would join in eventually. Finding the opportunity to speak alone, in his own language, she was able to ascertain that it was the wearing of just vest and pants that upset him, so he did not like PE. No concessions were possible on kit in this school.

Similarly, Gazala (also on an infant practice) encountered an incident where a teacher was reprimanding a distressed Muslim child, again about kit. There were no kit concessions. Track suits were not allowed. 'The teacher said track suit trousers were dangerous in gymnastics because they can catch on the apparatus.' Although Gazala wanted to intervene, to discuss religious requirements and possible feelings of guilt and embarrassment being induced in some Muslim children by such inflexibility, she felt powerless in the school-experience situation. In all of these cases the Muslim women did not want to risk confrontation that might jeopardize a 'pass' and consequently they chose non-confrontational paths, a kind of 'identity stasis' (Menter 1989). The women shared a 'silent empathy' with the Muslim children, growing angry with apparently inflexible systems that seemed to be alienating and excluding when a solution was so simple. This anger grew in the group interview situation:

> [Teachers] lead you to believe this is the law and part of the National Curriculum – what children have to wear ... if it's [just] school policy we might be able to ask for changes.
>
> (Nawar)

Schools often missed the opportunity to acknowledge the cultural affinity these student teachers shared with many of their pupils, the understanding they embodied, the knowledge they could bring to the whole-school situation and the bilingual skills that would improve the school lives of some young children.

Muslim Teachers' Perspectives of PE

The Muslim women who continued in my research project once qualified experienced the traumas of any young teacher in the early stages of such a demanding profession. In addition, the hijab-wearing teachers sometimes experienced difficult encounters with colleagues and senior managers related to their religious identity. It was not the degree to which the school community mirrored their identity that resulted in them feeling valued and included or side-lined and excluded. It was the attitudes of others towards Islam, subtly or vehemently directed at the visibly Muslim teachers in conversations, actions or glances, that led some to a state of 'identity stasis' in which they withdrew from any overt communication related to Islam whilst in the school context. This also meant that they kept their own Islamic lifestyle preferences and practices to themselves, increasing feelings of isolation and 'not belonging'. For those who could not cope with consciously splitting or denying their identity in this way, teaching in the state system became impossible. Despite some participants teaching in schools with large percentages of Muslim pupils, being able to build strong and positive relationships with the local community, this did not equate, in the eyes of the Muslim teachers, with the significance of sometimes less positive relations with colleagues and senior managers. This does little to change Sarwar's scepticism:

> It is sad that even in schools with 90%+ Muslim pupils there are few, if any, Muslim head teachers, teachers or non-teaching staff. This is often explained away as being due to a shortage of qualified people.
>
> (Sarwar 1994, 23)

129

It is important to recognize this wider context because it puts the physical education experiences encountered by the Muslim women in this research into perspective. The teaching of PE did become a much more private and therefore preferable activity to that encountered in training. Confidence grew in the teaching situation but not through processes of support and monitoring, rather through 'being left alone' to learn through experience, with no questions asked. One participant admitted that it took her two years to get the gymnastic apparatus out with her class. Time was a factor but so was lack of confidence to 'take the plunge'. Many primary teachers in their early careers will empathize with this insecurity. Another shared the fact that the threat of 'missing their PE lesson' was the most effective behaviour sanction in her classroom. It was not just PE that 'suffered' through being side-lined for the increasing accountability pressures on core subjects. Another Muslim teacher did not teach music for a whole year, not through Islamic concerns but because she was pressed so hard to produce good test results in numeracy and literacy. That this was not picked-up by the mentor or senior management is indicative of a reality inside hard-pressed primary schools.

The predominantly female nature of primary schools, particularly infant departments, suited some of the Muslim women. Those who could be described as 'most practising' in terms of commitment to religious adherence, experienced the greatest conflicts of conscience. Some expressed concerns about ten- and eleven-year-old pupils, already moving through puberty, having to change in mixed-sex public classroom situations. Others were concerned about 'sending the wrong messages' to the Muslim parents of the children in their schools if they taught subjects where there is no consensus within Islam. Others did not find this problematic. 'I am a teacher, that is my role and I just get on with it.' It is important to recognize that the Muslim women were differentially affected by their experiences in schools.

Higher Education PE Tutor's Perspective of PE and Islam

I became head of a department that had recently been asked to address the concerns of the Muslim women about their PE experiences. It was essential that I listened and responded to the problems if the College was going to retain and encourage these students into the teaching profession. Despite the liberal intention of introducing Islamic studies as a deliberate act to encourage more ethnic minority students into teacher training, the growing Muslim community did not always find the environment conducive. Over time, as a result of issues raised by the students and a process of negotiated change with senior management, the following changes were implemented: provision of single-sex accommodation, a prayer room, dietary requirements and the honouring of Festival days.

In addition, practices in PE had to change. The Muslim students had been expected to take part in the traditional course practices that had evolved. They were taught in mixed-sex groups with no concern for same-sex tutors. The public nature of PE spaces like the pool caused anxiety for some Muslim students. Some objected to contact activities in mixed-sex sessions and requests to remove the hijab in gymnastics for safety reasons. As a result of an on-going process of dialogue and negotiation change occurred (Benn 1996).

Muslim women were given the option of single-sex groups for PE, with same-sex staff (it was not the preferred choice of all Muslims), flexibility on dress for PE was emphasized with the inclusion of the hijab for those who wished, provided it was safely secured. Environments were made as private as possible, with same-sex environments being guaranteed in the pool. Staff became more sensitive in their teaching, for example in choice of themes and music selected in dance. Where a private, single-sex environment could not be guaranteed in swimming, a change of methodology was successful, using the Muslim women who could not enter the water as 'assistant teachers' on the pool-side. Since the course emphasis was on developing students' knowledge and confidence as teachers this was a successful extension of normal course practice. Similarly, having local classes 'in' to College during gymnastics in order to give students 'team-teaching' experiences enabled the Muslim students to participate more fully.

The case of Muslim men and boys was not studied in this research but it is recognized that their needs parallel those of Muslim women, though their disadvantaged position is not as contentious (Jawad 1998). At a recent opportunity to share my research with students and staff of another university, which has yet to address the needs of Muslim students, two Muslim men who were studying to become PE teachers approached me after the session. Our poignant exchange warrants inclusion at this point. They felt an affinity with everything they had heard and, being such a minority, wondered how they might address such issues in their own institution, or even if they had such a right to expect the accommodation of their religious requirements. Since Muslim men are required to cover the body from navel to knee the compulsory wearing of swimming trunks was problematic for them. Their participation in dance had presented some conflicts of conscience initially, interpreted as 'a lazy or disinterested attitude' instead of rooted in religious anxiety. Finally, the gym store-room had been used for their prayer in snatched moments when privacy could be assured. It seems there is a research project waiting to happen. Some researchers, such as McGuire and Collins (1998), have addressed important issues in relation to sports/PE participation by Asian heritage boys, but conflation of 'Asian' and 'Muslim' can be misleading. Not all Asian heritage boys are Muslim and not all Muslims are of Asian heritage.

Summary

Knowledge of Islamic religious requirements and the implications for PE is not new. The consensus of themes emerging, across and through the perspectives of PE recounted, will not surprise many but they are hopefully more vivid and meaningful because they come from lived experiences. It is clear from the accounts shared here that schools and institutions of higher education can be inclusive or exclusive in their policies and practices. It is not difficult to see how accusations of unintended, unwitting institutional racism can be attributed to practices long taken for granted in traditional physical education. Yet it is not in the gift of reified 'institutions' to move in the much needed direction towards 'valuing cultural diversity' (MacPherson Report 1999). It is within the attitudes and actions of every individual to make education a more welcoming, less hostile place for some minority groups. This means critical appraisal of policies and practice and positive change.

The Value and Potential of Research to Inform Practice

I hope that the experiences and accounts provided have demonstrated that research offers a rare opportunity to listen to much under-represented groups and to acknowledge the shortcomings in, and of, our established and current practices. In particular we have seen that:

- in some schools the needs of Muslim pupils in PE have been met and all children enjoy the many benefits of the subject;
- in some schools the needs of Muslim pupils in PE have not been addressed;
- some Muslim pupils experience guilt and distress in PE, even at primary level, which counters aims for lifelong participation and enjoyment in physical activity;
- in most schools the needs of Muslim teachers are not even on the agenda;
- Muslim teachers are sometimes subjected to religious prejudice and discrimination which excludes them from full participation in a profession which needs them;
- higher education has a key role in encouraging Muslim students into teaching and of increasing understanding of cultural diversity.

The research has also provided a clear basis from which to develop recommendations for moves towards greater inclusion:

- recognition that PE and Islam share a concern for health, exercise, and a balanced education for boys and girls;
- education of some 'gatekeepers' in the state system to spread greater awareness of positive images of Islam. This will counter media-fuelled islamophobia so damaging to attitudes and behaviour affecting both Muslim pupils and teachers;
- education about the value of PE and dance *in the education context*, would be helpful in some Muslim communities where there is uncertainty about intention or purpose;

- recognition that it is not *participation* in physical activities that raises te' with some sectors of the Muslim community but issues related to re.__ requirements being met. Where change is required, prioritizing inclusion in participation is a sound guiding principle;
- change in policy on areas such as kit, changing procedure and timing of clubs might be possible to accommodate religious requirements. In dance, sensitive selection of themes, music and performance situations, avoiding display of the body open to misinterpretation, would be helpful where tensions exist;
- local negotiation with Muslim communities is sometimes preferable to centralized policy since particular concerns can be addressed;
- further research into Islam and the position of boys/girls, men/women in PE/sports contexts can only be beneficial in adding knowledge to this area.

In conclusion, this research has other and important implications for professionals across sites, including those working in initial teacher training, mentor training and continuing professional development. Action, and co-ordinated action is needed in all of these arenas if physical education is to genuinely 'make a difference' to this currently marginalized group. As educators we need to be aware of the disadvantage certain practices perpetuate but also our potential to 'make a difference'. The simplest gesture can be highly significant. For example, allowing the wearing of a track suit, so enabling religious requirements for modesty of dress to be met, can hold the key to enjoying or hating the subject; feeling 'included' or 'excluded'; 'part of' or 'alienated from' a system where the undisputed priority should be that of *participating*. The PE inclusion statement in the latest consultation document for the National Curriculum 2000 (QCA 1999, 170) is to be celebrated. It adds a new dimension and directive for teachers to provide appropriate provision for 'pupils with specific religious and cultural beliefs and practices' at times of fasting, in relation to clothing, settings and groupings. This is a positive step in the right direction and it is hoped that a brighter future for many Muslim pupils, amongst others, will be built on this commitment.

References

Ahmed, L. (1992) *Women and Gender in Islam*. London: Yale University Press.
Benn, T. (1996) 'Muslim women and physical education in initial teacher training', *Sport, Education and Society* 1, 1, 5–21.
——(1998) 'Exploring experiences of a group of British Muslim women in initial teacher training and their early teaching careers', PhD thesis. Loughborough University.
Carrington, B. and Williams, T. (1988) 'Patriarchy and ethnicity: the link between school and physical education and community leisure activities', in J. Evans (ed.) *Teachers, Teaching and Control in Physical Education*. London: Falmer Press, 83–96.

Carroll, B. and Hollinshead, G. (1993) 'Equal opportunities: race and gender in physical education: a case study', in J. Evans (ed.) *Equality, Education and Physical Education*. London: Falmer Press, 154–69.

DfE (1995) *Physical Education in the National Curriculum*. London: HMSO.

Daiman, S. (1995) 'Women in sport in Islam', *Journal of the International Council for Health, Physical Education, Recreation, Sport and Dance* 32, 1, 18–21.

De Knop, P., Theeboom, M., Wittock, H. and De Martelaer, K (1996) 'Implications of Islam on Muslim girls' sports participation in western Europe', *Sport, Education and Society* 1, 2, 147–64.

Evans, J. (ed.) (1988) *Teachers, Teaching and Control in Physical Education*. London: Falmer Press.

Evans, J., Davies, B. and Penney, D. (1996) 'Back to the future: education policy and physical education', in N. Armstrong (ed.) *New Directions in Physical Education: Change and innovation*. London, Cassell Educational, 1–18.

Figueroa, P. (1993) 'Equality, multiculturalism, antiracism and physical education in the National Curriculum', in J. Evans (ed.) *Equality, Education and Physical Education*. London: Falmer Press.

Hargreaves, J. (1986) *Sport, Power and Culture*. Oxford: Polity Press.

——(1994) *Sporting Females*. London: Routledge.

Haw, K. (1998) *Educating Muslim Girls: Shifting discourses*. Buckingham: Open University Press.

Jawad, H. (1998) *The Rights of Women in Islam: An authentic approach*. London: Macmillan.

Kamiyole, I.O. (1986) 'Physical education in a Muslim culture', *International Journal of Physical Education* 23, 1, 22–9.

——(1993) 'Physical educators' albatross in African Muslim societies', *International Journal for Physical Education* 30, 28–31.

Kandiyoti, D. (1992) 'Women, Islam and the state: a comparative approach', in R. Juan and I. Coole (eds) *Comparing Muslim Societies*. Michigan: University of Michigan Press.

Laws, C. (1996) 'New directions for physical education teacher education in England and Wales', in N. Armstrong (ed.) *New Directions in Physical Education: Change and innovation*. London: Cassell Educational, 179–88.

Macpherson, W. (1999) *The Stephen Lawrence Inquiry: Report of an inquiry by Sir William Macpherson of Cluny*.London: The Stationery Office.

Mawdudi, A. (1989) *Towards Understanding Islam*. Leicester, Islamic Foundation.

McGuire, B. (1998) 'Problem page', Primary PE Focus, Autumn, PEAUK

Mcguire, B. and Collins, D. (1998) 'Sport, ethnicity and racism: the experience of Asian heritage boys', *Sport, Education and Society* 3, 1, 79–88.

Menter, I. (1989) 'Teaching practice stasis : racism, sexism and school experience in initial teacher education, *British Journal of Sociology of Education* 10, 4, 459–73.

Naciri, M. (1973) 'The Islamic position in sport', in *Sport in the Modern World – Chances and Problems*. Scientific Congress, Munich Olympics. Berlin, Springer Verlag, 599–601.

Ofsted (1999) *Raising the Attainment of Minority Ethnic Pupils: School and LEA responses*. London: Ofsted.

Parker-Jenkins, M. (1995) *Children of Islam*. Stoke-on-Trent: Trentham Books.

Penney, D. and Evans, J. (1999) *Politics, Policy and Practice in Physical Education*. London: E&F Spon.

QCA (1999) *The Review of the National Curriculum in England. The consultation material*. London: Qualifications and Curriculum Authority.

Runnymede Trust (1997) *Islamophobia: A challenge for all of us*. London: Runnymede Trust.

Samad, Y. (1998) 'Editorial: Muslim identities, Islam and Europe', *Innovation* 11, 4, 373–5.

Sarwar, G. (1994) *British Muslims and Schools*. London: Muslim Education Trust.

Sfeir, L. (1985) 'The status of Muslim women in sport: conflict between cultural traditions and modernisation, *International Review for Sociology of Sport* 20, 4, 283–304.

Siraj-Blatchford, I. (1993) 'Ethnicity and conflict in physical education: a critique of Carroll and Hollinsheads' case study', *British Educational Research Review* 19, 1, 77–82.

Sparkes, A. (1990) 'Winners, losers and the myth of rational change in physical education: towards an understanding of interests and power in innovation', in D. Kirk and R. Tinning (eds) *Physical Education Curriculum and Culture*. London: Falmer.

Talbot, M. (1990) 'Equal opportunities in physical education, in N. Armstrong (ed.) *New Directions in Physical Education*, vol. 1. London, Human Kinetics, 101–20.

Zouabi, M. (1975) 'Physical education and sport in Tunisia', *International Review of Sport Sociology* 10, 3–4, 109–14.

Contributors

Gill Bailey is a primary school teacher in Wolverhampton. She has taught across the primary age-range for more than twenty years, but much of her recent career has been spent teaching children in reception classes.

Julie Bedward is a qualitative researcher who has conducted several major studies as a Research Fellow at the University of Birmingham since 1987. She is currently working on several projects in the School of Education: an evaluation of an Emotional and Behavioural Difficulties unit, the development of an evaluation framework for clinical supervision and a study of gender differences in learning.

Tansin Benn is Senior Lecturer at the University of Birmingham, Westhill. She is Head of the Physical Education, Sport Studies and Dance Department. Her teaching and research interests cross arts, sport and teaching boundaries.

John Evans is Professor of Physical Education and Head of the Department of Physical Education, Sports Science and Recreation Management at Loughborough University. With Dawn Penney he has led the development of research centring upon policy and curriculum development and equity in physical education and, specifically, the National Curriculum for Physical Education.

Dawn Penney is a Senior Research Fellow in the Department of Physical Education, Sports Science and Recreation Management at Loughborough University where, with John Evans, she has led the development of research centring upon policy and curriculum development and equity in physical education and, specifically, the National Curriculum for Physical Education.

Susan Piotrowski is the Dean of Students at Canterbury Christ Church University College where, previously, she was a Principal Lecturer in Sport Science and Physical Education. She has a PhD in Philosophy from the University of London. Her publications include joint-authored contributions to *Sport Education and Society* and the *British Journal of New Zealand Studies*.

Carole Raymond has been involved in initial teacher training and in the professional development of experienced teachers for many years. More recently, she led the development of the partnership PGCE course and the training of subject mentors in physical education. She has published widely and her specialist interests include pedagogy, curriculum development and management.

Mike Sleap is a Lecturer in physical education and sport science at the University of Hull. He has conducted a number of projects concerned with young people and physical activity, notably the Happy Heart Project and the Fitness Challenge Project, and has published widely on the topic.

Peter Warburton is the Director of Sport at the University of Durham. He has a background in primary physical education and for the past ten years has edited the PEA UK publication 'Primary PE Focus'.

Michael Waring is Senior Lecturer in the School of Education at the University of Durham, where he lectures in PE and Sport.

Anne Williams is Professor and Head of the School of Education at King Alfred's College, Winchester and Honorary Senior Lecturer at the University of Birmingham. Her research interests include teacher education and physical education. She has published widely on primary school physical education and on gender issues in education as well as on the teacher education.

Jes Woodhouse is a Lecturer in Education (specializing in Physical Education) at the School of Education, the University of Birmingham. Prior to that he was an advisory teacher for physical education, during which time he co-ordinated a Sports Council/Dudley LEA National Demonstration Project aimed at developing physical education in the primary school.

Index